OUT OF SIGHT SPAIN
top 150 cool places to visit

Harry King

Cover design by Harry King. Painting of *Costa de Morte* (The Coast of Death) displayed at Faro de Estaca de Bares, Galicia.

First published in 2021 by Paragon Publishing, Rothersthorpe

ISBN 978-1-78222-815-8

Book design, layout and production management by Into Print
www.intoprint.net
+44 (0)1604 832149

ACKNOWLEDGEMENTS

My wife Joan and I have travelled the highways and byways of Spain for almost two decades. We have rested our heads in rural accommodation, under canvas and frequently became lost. *Out of Sight Spain* is the result of our experiences. While I wrote the book, Joan has frequently kept me on the straight and narrow, removing my long historic descriptions, deleting popular tourist spots, editing spelling mistakes and bad grammar. The book would never have been published without her help.

There are many pictures in this book. The majority have been taken by me, acquired through *Wikimedia Commons* and the Tourist Boards, or are available in the Public Domain. A small number of photos are credited (the chapter numbers are referenced too):

Annie Bungeroth 3, Escapadural 6, Van Gullivea 6, Pinterest 8 & 6, crazy tourist 13, Aralinfo 17, Ruize Quiroz 25, Ruta Industrial Heritage 25, Had Rentals 30, Cruceros Rias 34, Tarbus 34, Esainof 35, Smithonian 37, Ursula Wall 40, Absolute Avaruia 42, Schermopname 45, Sera Markoff 47, Pickfair 48, Reditt 49, Norman Millar 50, Culture Trip 69, Culture Map Dallas 59, Cronica Global el Espanol 73, Diary Almeria 74, Totenart 76, Eye on Spain 77. Images Relacionadas 78.

CONTENTS

OLD TIMES

RECENT TIMES

WARS

FROM THE LAND

PREFACE

Embrace visible history gradually degrading in days gone by. Men gathered in a town square. Women laughing by a fountain. Children playing with a ball. Little by little, nature is recovering its past. Weeds appear in streets. Walls tumble down into a pile of rubble. And for some reason these places are fascinating.

Can you imagine these intriguing places which were part of the fabric of Spain many years ago; still visible to explorers who wish to find them? Can you imagine being a Roman or a Moor, to hear gunfire and feel fear in death? How about life as a peasant farmer or a modern-day politician squandering EU grants? Consider gnarled fishermen on the wild Coast of Death or even Cervantes wandering around La Mancha.

Covering relics of old times, picturesque ghost towns and a different perspective on big cities, Out of Sight Spain shows the way to cool, unusual, often well-hidden places. Clamber over long forgotten ruins, or hike on some remote trail, or even go underground in mines and sewers. Contemplate the artifacts of land sea and air. Visit vestiges of the Civil War. Get underneath the skin of well-known cities. Stand on a faded Olympic diving board. Understand the bricks and mortar of economic mismanagement. Finally, enjoy some traditional gastronomy along the way.

A word of warning. Almost 70 million people visit Spain each year, different nationalities and different personalities, enjoying what the tourism superpower Spain has to offer. Popular images of sun, sea and sand, art in Madrid, Las Fallas in Valencia, a pilgrimage to Santiago de Compostela, running with bulls in Pamplona, flamenco in Sevilla, heavenly beaches, tomato hurling in La Tomatina and a hectic night life. These activities are all described in good visitor guides... but not here in this book.

OLD TIMES

1. CUENCA ENCANTADA
enchanted erosion

THE CITY OF CUENCA'S MOST EMBLAMIC IMAGE IS ITS HANGING HOUSES, not just hanging but defying gravity, their cantilevered wooden balconies and barred windows looking over a gap carved by the Jucar and Huecar rivers in a vertiginous gorge below. In a feat of extreme engineering these houses are made of masonry, seated on projecting beams set in a rock wall.

On the other side of the Hanging Houses, and complying with the noble art of wandering, stretches the central Calle Alfonso VIII, a mosaic of colourful facades of stately homes, many of which are now converted into charming hotels and pricy shops selling traditional products. The Plaza Mangana is not to be missed either, with a spiky tower of the same name and a clock that marks the city's time. Terraces that animate the San Miguel neighbourhood, behind the Plaza Mayor are reached by a kind of secret underworld of stairways, passageways and alleys.

Cuenca is an incredibly old historic city best explored with the help of visitor literature. Of that there is plenty. Ciudad Encantada is even older, but not man made. Ciudad Encantada is a geological fantasy of eroded wonders near Cuenca that has been sculpted by water and wind over millions of years.

Located near the town of Valdecabras, in the heart of the Serrania de Cuenca Natural Park and surrounded by immense pine forests, its origin dates to 90 million years ago, when the Enchanted City was part of the Thetis seabed. Calm waters led to a deposit of salts, especially calcium carbonate. The sea withdrew and a seabed of limestone, emerged to the surface. Thousands of years of action by rain, wind and ice means today we can contemplate this impressive karst phenomenon which is defined as a 'landscape of limestone which has been eroded by dissolution, producing ridges, towers, fissures, sinkholes and other characteristic landforms.'

Visiting this enchanted formations consists of taking a circular route of approximately three kilometres, perfectly signposted. During an hour and a half, a variety of rock formations, which have been given names of animals and objects, come into view. At each of them there is a lectern with detailed information. The heterogeneity of the rocks, in terms of their chemical composition and degree of hardness, has allowed an uneven wear resulting in a surprising display of picturesque art.

Lastly 'encantada' in Spanish means delighted (e.g., to meet you). It also means haunted or bewitched.

EL TORCAL DE ANTEQUERA NATURAL AREA, in the heart of southern Spain, is another spectacular karst landscape which holds sinkholes, shaped rock formations and circular depressions.

This stone city, which is much more rugged than Cuenca Encantada, has a network of well signposted hiking trails. It is advisable to follow these marked trails to avoid disorientation in this stone maze. Walking these routes at a cool 1,000 metres gives contact with nature while enjoying its whimsical designs.

LOCATIONS

Valdecabras, Castilla La Mancha.
Map reference 40 0936 N, 2 0205 W.
Nearest large town – Cuenca

El Torcal de Antequera, Province of Malaga.
Map reference 36 5707 N, 4 3222 W.
Nearest large town – Malaga.

2. LEGACY OF THE CELTS
Castro de Santa Tecla

WHAT IS A CASTRO – THESE STRANGE CIRCULAR BUILDINGS HUDDLED CLOSE TOGETHER? A Castro is a village inhabited from the 1st century BC, lacking straight streets or corners. The road network and houses were all circular. The earliest circular houses at Santa Tecla were made solely from straw-mud; the latest, which can be seen today, were built with masonry. The roof was made of branches and mud set over long poles, wigwam style. There was no central support pole. Castro's were located in naturally protected areas; high up, near rivers or small peninsulas, close to water sources, arable land, and even higher areas for grazing livestock.

Castro de Santa Tecla are well-preserved ruins. Two buildings have been rebuilt to give an idea of how people lived here. According to historians, houses and entire villages were built in round shapes since, according to their Celtic mythology, there were no corners to hold spirits.

Santa Tecla is an archaeological site located on the Santa Tecla mountain, close to the municipality of La Guardia. From here you can see Spain, Portugal, the mouth of the Mino estuary and the Atlantic Ocean. At 344 metres high, it is a privileged place to be. However, on this cool Atlantic coast and because of its height, there is a lot of fog around.

Castro de Santa Tecla was inhabited an exceedingly long time ago but went into decline leading up to 4th century AD, these dates being established from materials found in various archaeological digs. Its inhabitants were dedicated mainly to agriculture, livestock, fishing, and shell fishing. Fields were cultivated one kilometre away from the Castro,

although aerial photography has shown terraced areas in the forest that perhaps were used for planting crops.

No ditches, parapets or embankments have been found indicating little need for defence. Perhaps its strategic location in the mountain, next to the mouth of the Mino river, was enough to feel safe. This Castro also enjoyed a system for channelling rainwater through drains carved into the rock under the pavement of its circular streets.

Wandering around this site, between circular houses with no obvious streets, may seem a bit chaotic. But look for petroglyphs! What is that you may well ask? Scattered around Santa Tecla are remains of previous occupiers, probably from 2000 BC, as evidenced by various rock engravings, many of them underneath Castro houses.

This place was abandoned until the ruins were re discovered in 1862. Now all you have to do is get there. But a warning, although accessible by car almost to the top of the hill, there is not a lot of parking. A walk up a road, then a track, and even a long flight of steps, is necessary to enter the site.

YET ANOTHER CASTRO IS TO BE FOUND AT NEARBY BARONA. This Castro too is in a striking location, next to the sea on a peninsula. A forest, waves crashing into the sand, soaring birds and among this - a Castro. Its inhabitants lived from the sea, with a diet rich in fish and shellfish. Many hooks and fishing tools have been found.

Twenty houses were built here, family homes of different sizes, circular and oval in shape, without windows or doors. A fort too, its well-preserved entrance guarded by a double defensive wall of stone and sand, with a moat four metres wide and three metres deep which allowed defence against any attacker.

LOCATIONS – both close to each other
   Castro Santa Tecla, Galicia.
   Map reference 41 5328 N, 8 5204 W.
   Nearest large town – Vigo
   Barona, Galicia.
   Map reference 42 4135 N, 9 0108 W.
   Nearest large town - Ponteverda

3. LEGACY OF THE ROMANS
feel these ancient times

IT WAS THE ROMANS AND LATER THE MUSLIMS WHO SHAPED HISPANIA'S CULTURAL HERITAGE. After ousting the Carthaginians in the 3rd century B.C., the Romans flourished for 400 years. Rome's rulers allowed Romans and Hispanics to intermarry. Under Roman rule Hispania's economy grew, supplying the rest of its empire with grains, wool, olive oil, fruits and wood.

The Iberian Peninsula was a major challenge to Roman engineers, a good example of how to overcome big natural obstacles. The design and construction of Roman roads was based on finding the fastest and most direct transit possible between two main points in order to mobilise troops and move goods. Major roads, exemplified by the Via Augusta were connected to secondary roads, which then led to new population centres. It's very unlikely the Roman empire would have survived as long as it did without such networks. Many highways in Spain now go over old Roman roads. That's why we have a phrase, 'All roads lead to Rome.'

Aqueducts, incredible works of civil engineering were built to provide water to sustain urban populations. Still standing are the aqueduct at Segovia, Les Ferreres aqueduct in Tarragona and the Aqueduct de los Milagros in Merida Extremadura. The Romans built amphitheatres for spectacles and sports such as Santiponce, Merida, Tarragona and Segobriga; and theatres at Merida, Malaga, Medellín and Zaragoza. There are many original Roman bridges still standing, but many have been restored or strengthened, it's difficult to tell how 'Roman' they are now. Still standing are the Roman bridges at Cordoba, Merida, Salamanca and Alcantara. Many medieval walls of Roman origin exist at Lugo, Zaragoza and Tarragona.

THERE IS EVIDENCE OF ROMANS ALL ACROSS SPAIN. A Roman theatre in Cartagena. The Tower of Hercules in Coruna. However, Segovia a small city northeast of Madrid, delivers more 'wow' than many other historic centres. How many cities are split down the middle by an enormous ancient Roman aqueduct? Dated back to the 81-96 AD reign of Emperor Domitian, this granite structure has 167 arches which have been rebuilt and proudly maintained over the centuries It is now a symbol of Segovia. This aqueduct is widely considered the most well-preserved of its kind in Spain. It is in such good condition today that it is still used to transport water, albeit in modern day pipes, which run along original water ducts. As you would expect, this city is also 'awash' with artefacts and remains from various time periods.

RUNNING SERGOVIA CLOSE ARE THE RUINS OF MERIDA IN EXTREMADURA which were awarded UNESCO World Heritage Status in 1993 owing to its outstanding Roman archaeology. Although inhabited since prehistoric times, the Romans founded the city, then called Emerita Augusta, back in 25BC which went on to be one of the most important places in the Empire. Of the many ruins visible today, the triumphal arch, theatre and aqueduct are particularly noteworthy.

WELL OFF THE BEATEN TRACK WE HAVE LUGO, SITTING IN COOL, SPLENDID ISOLATION in the north eastern province of Galicia. A distinctive, visible remnant of the Roman presence is the impressive, fortified wall which guards the city and makes Lugo the only European city still entirely surrounded by a Roman wall. There are some 71 towers along the way in this UNESCO World Heritage Site, all giving excellent views of the city.

AWAY FROM VISITOR ROUTES, BAELO CLAUDIO IS ONLY SOME 20 KM FROM WINDY TARIFA. Baelo Claudia was once an important point of trade with Africa. The town prospered thanks to its salted fish trade but was severely damaged by an earthquake in the 2nd century. Nonetheless, the Roman remains on display here are some of the  most complete and well-preserved in Spain. They include ancient gates into the city, a theatre, thermal baths, a market, and a paved forum.

THE HIDDEN PORT OF SAGUNTO WAS FOR MANY YEARS, MORE IMPORTANT than the nearby city of Valencia. The town boasts an impressive 1st century theatre, remains of Roman bridges and other quayside structures. Many Jewish, Moorish, and Roman remains can be found here. Imagine life during the reign of the Romans? Standing in this port, or among the ruins of an old palace or theatre, or next to a wall or aqueduct, or on an old road - just feel these ancient times.

LOCATIONS

Sergovia, Province of Sergovia.
Map reference 40 5635 N, 4 0631 W.
Nearest large town - Madrid.

Merida, Extremadura.
Map reference 38 5508 N, 6 2104 W.
Nearest large town - Badajoz.

Lugo, Galicia.
Map reference 43 0036 N, 7 3324 W.
Nearest large town - Coruna.

Baelo Claudio, Cadiz Province.
Map reference 36 0523 N, 5 4630 W.
Nearest large town - Algeciras.

Sagunto, Valencia Province.
Map reference 39 4048 N, 0 1642 W.
Nearest large town - Valencia.

4. LEGACY OF THE MOORS
their eyes shone like burning candles

IN 711 HE LED A STRONG MUSLIM ARMY ACROSS THE STRAITS OF GIBRALTAR FROM MOROCCO. Tariq Ibn Ziyad quickly defeated the ruling Visigoth forces and faced little resistance in taking control of their capital, Toledo. With the additional fall of Cordoba an Islamic state known as 'Al-Andalus' was born under direct control of Damascus, the capital of the Islamic world. Only a few years later the Christian Reconquest began in the mountains of Asturias and a 700-year battle began to evict the occupiers. But it wasn't until 1492 that the Christian Reconquest was complete when the city of Granada was retaken.

This snippet of history can be used to explain the 'Moros y Cristianos' festivals which take place across Spain every year. Locals dress up, as either Moors or Christians, to enact battle scenes between two groups who fought during the Reconquest. If only able to visit one festival, then it must be at Alcoy in the province of Alicante which commemorates the Battle of Alcoy in 1275 when St George helped defeat the Moorish forces led by Al Azraq.

Although there is no attempt to achieve historical accuracy, this is one of Spain's great festivals. Noise, colour, and fun abound as Christian and Moorish armies march around town all day accompanied by their own bands. The Spanish love of fireworks is evident during this fiesta when the city is covered with a fog of gunpowder. Balconies are decorated with the red cross flag of St George.

Let's wind the clock back! The European scholar Edward Scobie, sympathetic to Spaniards, remembered the Moorish conquest this way. 'The reins of the Moors horses were as fire, their faces black as pitch, their eyes shone like burning candles, their horses were swift as leopards and riders fiercer than a wolf in a sheepfold at night. The noble Goths were broken in an hour, quicker than tongue can tell. Oh, luckless Spain!'

Rule by the Moors, as Muslims came to be known, involved plenty of brutality – most conquests do. There were certainly periods of repression under some emirs and sultans such as massacres and forced conversion to Islam. Yet the Al-Andalus which evolved became in many ways Europe's most advanced, tolerant, and literate society. Muslims were in charge but allowed their Christian and Jewish subjects autonomy to practice their own religion and go about their

lives relatively unmolested. It's misleading to romanticise and idealise this 'golden age' too much, nonetheless, during these centuries Cordoba did become Europe's largest and most advanced city alongside today's most distinguished cities of Andalusia, such as Seville and Granada.

Even after the last Moors were expelled in 1492, they left their mark on Spain in countless ways. The introduction of language and education taught in schools, libraries, and universities. A numbering system used today replacing the clumsy Roman numerals. An introduction of astronomical tables and a primitive sextant to measure latitude. Advances in maths and medicine. New agricultural practices with different crops from China. The manufacture of silk and paper. An African cuisine. And last but not least, the creative, stunning architecture in Cordoba.

THE MOORS LEFT BEHIND THE SUMPTIOUS PLACE OF GRANADA, the Alhambra and particularly Cordoba's grand mosque the Mezquita, with its picturesque Jewish Quarter, and the Medina Azahara palace complex. Castles, baths, and other remains are scattered all across Spain. In short, Spain wouldn't be Spain without Al-Andalus.

Some people think if they have seen one Moorish palace then they have seen them all. Not true. Scheduling a visit to the Alhambra in Granada should be on everyone's 'Top Things to Do in Spain.' It may not be 'out of sight' but it is certainly different. Constructed on a plateau overlooking the city of Granada, hundreds and hundreds of years of history have passed through this palace. The Alhambra after the expulsion of the Moors had much of its interior defaced, furniture ruined, and tiling removed. What followed was restoration, wars, earthquakes, and even more restoration which is still 'work in progress' today.

SOME PEACEFUL MOORS WERE LEFT BEHIND IN THE AFTERMATH OF THE RECONQUEST. From rulers to ruled, from victors to vanquished, from Islamic Moors to converted Christians. They built tracks in inaccessible locations. Mozarabic is a term used to describe these narrow-stepped trails which cross over mountains from valley to valley. They are true marvels of engineering zigzagging down into the depths of the deepest ravines and up the other side. Trails characterised by thousands and thousands of steps with supporting walls in tricky places. Many have withstood the ravages of time albeit with a lack of maintenance. They can be seen at Benimelli, in the Val de Laguart. Here you'll be stepping down through a stunning valley of almond, cherry, and orange groves, surrounded by peace and tranquillity, to an imposing location called the Baranco del Infierno.

LOCATIONS

Alcoy, Alicante Province.
Map Reference 38 4156 N, 0 2352 W.
Nearest large town - Gandia

Granada, Province of Granada.
Map reference 37 0139 N, 3 3602 N.
Nearest large town - Malaga.

Benimelli, Province of Valencia.
Map reference 38 5019 N, 0 0207 N.
Nearest large town - Pego or Denia.

5. ON HIGH CRAGS
Denia, Alicante, Xativa and Coco castles

ALTHOUGH IT IS THOUGHT THERE WERE OVER 10,000 CASTLES IN SPAIN, today only about 2500 remain, and the number that can be visited is far less. Most castles in Spain are located in the region of Castille & Leon. Even the name of this region is derived from the word 'castle'. There are many castles in other regions too, constructed by the Romans, Moors or Christians when they conquered, or reposed, Iberian Peninsula territories.

Castles can be found on high crags, controlling an approach to fertile valleys, guarding strategic passes, or routes across the plains, protecting estuaries and coastal areas. Those on a hilltop use the high ground as part of their defence, those on plains were protected by deep and wide moats.

Castles served primarily to protect people and territory. Their function sometimes defensive against enemy forces, or offensive built by invading armies to consolidate gains and signal their intention to remain in newly conquered lands. Lack of centralised power during the early Middle Ages encouraged the proliferation of castle building by ambitious, often rebellious lords and princes. In these cases, they became symbols of success, status, and power.

We tend to think of castles simply in military terms, but they also helped to shape the social, economic and cultural life of people. Villages and towns frequently established themselves around castles, creating hubs to provide work for their inhabitants. In times of hostility, people would seek protection inside the castles. In return for protection, villagers often surrendered their freedom becoming vassals to the lord of the castle, creating one of the most identifiable social structures associated with this period: feudalism.

While Span's many castles are concentrated inland, there are costal castles too, built with a different purpose. Here are three and by common consent, the most impressive inland castle too.

DENIA IS A BEAUTIFUL MEDITERRANEAN PORT TOWN.

Its castle is an important landmark which can be seen from many kilometres out to sea. The Moors ruled Denia from the 8th to the 13th century. They built this mighty fortress against potential intruders. After they left, it crumbled for hundreds of years. A brief occupation by the French during the 19th century Peninsular War led to it being rebuilt.

Different civilizations have settled in the old town and Roman remains have been discovered, influencing its culture as we now know it. Arab influence can be found in the cuisine and various buildings in town. In fact, the name 'Denia' comes from 'Daniyah' which means 'lowland' in Arabic. Today the castle attracts people for its historical importance, architecture, and artifacts.

The castle involves a short, steep climb alongside a pretty street of coloured houses. An impressive arched entrance dates from Moorish times but the castle itself is a mixture of styles developed over the centuries. Originally built next to the sea, a plethora of modern life in the form of a dual carriage, shops, restaurants, and marina now means the sea is two hundred metres from the castle.

SANTA BARBARA CASTLE IS REACHED BY A TUNNEL AND LIFT FROM A MAIN ROAD.

Located in the heart of Alicante, it sits about 160 metres on top of a rocky hill. Such is the pace of modern life an underground station now lies deep below. One of the largest medieval fortresses in Spain, it's a fabulous place for exploring dungeons, cannons, towers, and a moat, while learning more about the people who lived there over the centuries.

The castle dates back to the 9th century and much of its magnificent architecture is the legacy of the Moors. After the Arabs, Alicante castle had a colourful past being captured by many different forces over time. It was twice in foreign hands. First the French in 1691 and then the English during the War of Spanish Succession. Gradually it became less important as a military base and in later years was a converted prison before being abandoned.

In the 1960s the castle was opened to the public. Visitors can take a leisurely walk around, have lunch or a snack in a restaurant and enjoy views over the city. In the summer, evening concerts are organised within the castle walls.

CASTILLO DE XATIVA IMPRESSES WITH ITS SIZE, SPREAD ALONG THE TOP OF A HILL and visible from kilometres away. For a defensive bastion, it's a perfect location. Although the Romans were the first to establish a fortification here, this hill has been coveted by every power-hungry ruler who's ever passed through the region - the Moors, the French, the Bourbons, the Hapsburgs and the Aragonese.

Inland from Gandia, the importance of the Xativa Castle lies in its strategic location, being near the Via Augusta, a Roman road crossing from Cadiz to Rome, via Cartagena, the Mediterranean coast, the Pyrenees and then down to Italy (the road appears in other Chapters in this book). The castle monitored and protected the Roman road.

Touring Xativa Castle is exhausting and takes a few hours. First a walk up a steep hill to the entrance gate. Turn towards the west to explore the smaller Castillo Menor, or east for the Castillo Mayor.

Start with Castillo Mayor: this is by far the more interesting of the two. Walking uphill the entire way, ancient gates, an Arabic fountain, a Catholic chapel, and old bronze cannons are passed. Look inside the private rooms of the castle's royal masters, explore dark confines of a prison which held illustrious convicts such as the Duque de Calabria, the King of Mallorca, and the brother of Saint Francis Borgia. All along the route are stunning views over Xativa and the countryside.

The Castillo Menor is also interesting; this is actually the older of the two fortifications, built in pre-Roman times by the region's original Iberian inhabitants. There are no significant sights here but strolling along ancient walls is absorbing and doesn't take too long.

BY COMMON CONSENT, CASTLE DE COCO IS ONE OF THE MOST IMPRESSIVE INLAND CASTLES. Located near Segovia it is huge and dominating; so solid it will never fall down. Though many castles in Spain were built in an Islamic style, the Castle of Coca is predominantly Christian in architecture, complete with an attractive exterior made entirely of huge bricks. It was built in the 15th century, a representation of undeniable luxury. The tan walls stand out amongst its surroundings. One of the most interesting points of this castle is the 40-foot-deep moat.

Spanish guidebooks offer many castles similar to Coco. Enormous, awesome, sometimes remote, well-preserved fairy-tale fortresses, usually on top of a hill.

LOCATIONS

Denia, Alicante Province.
Map reference 38 5019 N, 0 0618 W.
Nearest large town - Gandia.

Alicante, Alicante Province.
Map reference 38 2407 N, 0 2925 W. - Capital of region

Xativa, Valencia Province.
Map reference 38 5924 N, 0 3124 W.
Nearest large town - Gandia.

Coco, Sergovia Province.
Map reference 41 2154 N, 4 3131 W.
Nearest large town - Sergovia.

6. ABANDONED CURIOSITIES
tunnel, fort and mills

LA ENGANA TUNNEL - PART OF A PROPOSED SANTANDER TO MEDITERRANEAN RAILWAY LINE, was an attempt by the Spanish government to connect the Bay of Biscay with the Mediterranean Sea. Its construction underneath the Cantabrian mountains, lasted for over 17 years, from 1941 to 1959, employing hundreds of workers, including during the first few years, Republican prisoners. At the time of its construction, at almost 7 kilometres in length, it was the longest railway tunnel in Spain, but never fully completed. Until the arrival of the High-Speed train, La Engana was the longest tunnel in Spain.

For years, the tunnel was used by residents of the area; herders, recreational off-roaders, and truck drivers who found the mountain passes snowbound in winter. Sections of the structure collapsed in 1999 and 2005, so the southern entrance was walled up making it impassable for vehicles. Traveling inside the tunnel on foot is

extremely dangerous as there are ceiling-high piles of debris, some sections remain flooded, and there are concerns about a risk of further landslides. It is not unusual to find buildings in Spain which are never used. The Engana tunnel is yet another waste of money on a vanity project that ended abandoned.

THE FORT OF SAN CRISTOBAL WAS BUILT in the 19th century as a military fortress and used as a prison during the Franco regime. It is only a few kilometres from Pamplona. On May 22, 1938, 795 Republican prisoners fled from Fort San Cristóbal. It was the scene of the largest

prison escape in the history of Spain. 221 died in the attempt. There were 2,497 inmates in the old fortress at the time. In 1998, after being used by the army, it was closed permanently.

NOWHERE CAN YOU FIND A COLLECTION OF 60 MILLS IN ONE LOCATION

except the mills on the slopes of Monte Campo do Couto, in the Spanish municipality of El Rosal, Galicia. These mills, built during the 18th century, were arranged in a cascade so that they could share the same water channel. Energy provided by water as it flowed down the mountain was utilized to grind corn and wheat. Although no longer operational, the beautifully restored mills offer great cultural heritage to the region.

The mills are built in two groups. The first group called the Folon Mills, consist of 36 mills located on the slope of the Folon, over a stream also called Folon. The second group called Picon Mills, consist of 24 mills and are located nearby over a stream, unsurprisingly called the Picon. The simple buildings are squat, two story affairs that don't look

much on their own, but as they were built in a perfectly line down the hill, they really become something special.

Most of the mills are built from stone with the actual mill situated on the top floor while the ground floor is occupied by machinery driven by water. Some of them include an adjacent watering trough for animals. The oldest inscription on these structures dates back to 1702. It is said, the existence of these mills is probably linked to the influence of the monks at the nearby Santa María de Oia Monastery. Today they are seen as an amazing photo opportunity. At the time of building, the mills belonged to various villages as communal property; others were privately owned or shared among several families, and there were also some rented out.

In 1988, the Folon and Picon Mills were declared a site of cultural interest. Soon after work began to recover and restore the mills and their surroundings. Today, there is a well-marked, circular hiking trail in the area with the possibility of free guided tours to see and understand how these mills operate. It is always amazing when the needs of an industrial era end up producing a thing of beauty; the Mills of Folon and Picon are one of those happy accidents that shouldn't be missed.

LOCATIONS

La Engana Tunnel, Cantabria.
Map reference 43 0654 N, 3 4431 W.
Nearest large town - Santander.

Fort San Chistobal, Navarra.
Map reference 42 5116 N, 1 3950 W.
Nearest large town - Pamplona.

El Rosal, Galicia.
Map reference 41 5604 N, 8 5011 W.
Nearest large town – Vigo.

7. ABANDONED INDUSTRY
war and cement

PEOPLE WHO SPEND THEIR FREE TIME VISITING ABANDONED PLACES
call themselves urban explorers. They want to know what's inside a decaying building and experience the adrenaline rush that comes with exploration. Safety issues with decaying buildings exist, structural integrity and hazardous environmental issues too. Walls collapse, floors cave in, roofs leak, termites eat wood, steel rusts and people trip over hazards. These possibilities do not stop avid urban explorers.

The three abandoned factories featured here are protected from safety hazards by the Spanish authorities. Cleaned up, sanitized, they are safe to explore. They are all in northern Spain where sturdy old buildings crumble slowly.

HONTORIA DE LA CANTERA IS A NON-DESCRIPT SORT OF TOWN
located on the western slopes of a wooded hill, on the other side of which are the famous quarries which give the town its name. It is close to Burgos, next to the Soria highway. In these historical quarries stone was extracted to build monuments in the city of Burgos, including the 13th century cathedral. In fact, nearly all houses in Burgos are built with quarry limestone.

The bowels of Mount Hontoria de la Cantera hold arcane secrets. The openings left today are stark, dismal and gloomy, horrifying in the strict

sense of the word horror. Despite the passage of time, the rough floor of the quarry still smells of sulphur, it seems like the entrance to hell. Why? In 1937 the old mining operation became a powder keg for the Spanish Army. Franco used these artificial caves to store arms and ammunition. Here bullets, dynamite and people slept together.

Entering the powder keg is unsettling. It contains many mysteries. Penetrating inside, light fades, darkness takes over, complete disorientation occurs. Legends can still be heard in Hontoria. They say prisoners worked here to create more space in the huge cavern. Workshops, warehouses, and houses for troops were built in the 1940s and '50s. Part of the structure is still preserved, but extremely deteriorated and practically in ruins. Site operations were closed 1994 but it is now open safely to the public.

A MUNITIONS FACTORY AT ORBAITZETA WAS OPENED IN 1874 NEAR THE SPANISH / FRENCH BORDER. It closed 10 years later and since then only ruins remain. The arms factory and its surroundings have been declared a Site of Cultural Interest since 2007. If going to Navarra, information about the picturesque valley of Irati will appear in guidebooks. It is estimated that more than 150 families lived in the valley of Irati. However, not every book details the abandoned Munitions Factory, which is a great example of old industrial archelogy.

An arms factory in Orbaizeta does not surprise anyone who knows the history of this area. It was a conflict zone. The factory produced cannons, ammunition, and quality iron until the invention of Blast Furnaces at the end of the 19th century.

Today the building is abandoned. There are dilapidated walls, workshops, warehouses, ancient stoves and an impressive water tunnel. 150 years after opening, it is now covered in abundant vegetation.

FABRICA DE CENENTO DE XERALLO IS AN ABANDONED CEMENT FACTORY. Although difficult to find on a map try the Province of Lleida, in the foothills of the Pyrenees close to Andorra. With a need for cement to build reservoirs and roads, this cement factory was constructed. Xerallo was the best place to build it. There were limestone quarries nearby to supply raw material and it was close to the Malpas mines, to obtain coal for furnaces.

Its operatives came from post-war Andalusia. Many of them fleeing from hunger. Working conditions were harsh. The factory was built with picks and shovels. The material arrived on donkeys and mules through the mountains. Plant operators and their families lived in barracks because there were insufficient houses to accommodate people who had come to live in this rural depopulated region. The solution - rebuild the town with housing, canteen services, cinema, church, school, and health care. Despite the harshness of the climate, Xerallo was a new home for people who came with a dream of rebuilding their lives.

The Xerallo plant produced cement from 1950 until its closure in 1973. Low profitability they said! The impact of closure on this region, with extraordinarily little industry, was serious. It housed 388 citizens. After closure, the town was abandoned. Today, although empty, it is not quite a ghost town since some of its houses have been reformed into holiday homes.

LOCATIONS

Hontoria de la Cantera, Burgos.
Map reference 42 1102 N, 3 3833 W.
Nearest large town - Burgos.
Obraitzata, Navarra.
Map reference 42 5829 N, 1 1347 W.
Nearest large town - Pamplona.
Xerallo, Lleida.
Map reference 42 2209 N, 0 5151 W.
Nearest large place - Andorra

8. ABANDONED VILLAGES
Esco, Moya and more

ESCO WILL UNDOUBTEDLY FASCINATE LOVERS OF ABANDONED PLACES. Abandoned since it was expropriated during the 1960s for the construction of the Yesa Reservoir. Abandoned villages, even piles of stone, all have a special mysterious ghostly charm. Esco is no exception, leaving behind a history that seems lost to time.

Esco's history is long and rich. It is necessary to go back to the pre-Roman conquest of the 1st century BC to find its origin when the area was already inhabited by Jacetanos and Vascones. After a Roman presence, Esco acquired great strategic relevance, having a castle built at the beginning of the 13th century. It is located in the foothills of the Pyrenees between the borders of Zaragoza and Navarra.

In the middle of the 19th century there were around 250 inhabitants here. A century later, the aforementioned construction of the Yesa reservoir caused its gradual abandonment. A stroll between its buildings and crumbling walls is somewhat apocalyptic.

Today the town belongs to the Ebro Hydrographic Confederation, who for years have consistently denied requests to reverse the progressive degradation and to return it back to some form of habitation. Although it is on the route of the Camino de Santiago Path and declared a Historic Artistic Site, there is no political will to rehabilitate this small architectural jewel. Esco, is a sad example called 'Empty Spain', a country losing some of its best jewels of cultural heritage.

THE RUINS OF MOYA ARE BIG, EXPANSIVE AND DUSTY, variously described as the unknown city, the forgotten city, or the abandoned city. The City of Moya had a castle, two hospitals, two convents, seven parishes and eight access doors that opened up the way inside. It is strategically located at 1,155 metres above sea level, a high point from which any enemy could be seen. It was built for fighting and defence with two walls; barriers built as a response to violence proliferating at that time. After all an invading army, or a revolt by the population of the City, could at a stroke, deprive the Marquis of precious possessions.

With the passage of time, citizens who lived in the city moved to other neighbourhoods with easier access, or to establish new villages downhill. All that is left now are a couple of rows of ruined houses which were abandoned only in the 1950's and the odd vulture circling

lazily overhead. Why was the capital of the Marquesado de Moya, with more than 30 outlying villages abandoned? The castle and villages are all perched uncomfortably high above an extremely hot plain with little water. And there was no real purpose to its existence, only to serve the non-existent needs of a fighting castle.

PENARRUBIA, A TOWN AT THE BOTTOM OF A RESEVOIR NEAR MALAGA

is another case of submerged habitation. Penarrubia was drowned in an area called Guadalteba in 1971. Its 2,000 inhabitants were evicted to build the Teba reservoir. Their houses were destroyed except for a school, barracks, and a church. In times of drought its ruins can be seen, especially the church bell tower which still stands today.

ALCADIMA IS A SMALL ABANDONED TOWN EXCEEDINGLY DIFFICULT

TO FIND. No signs or directions, just secondary roads and along a long narrow dirt road full of sharp turns. To locate it, look between the municipalities of Lietor and Ayna.

Although Alcadima was depopulated some 50 years ago, there are still people who visit and care for the area. Some houses are in good condition, nestling in narrow alleys. Some of them are shut behind large wooden doors with old, rusted iron locks. Others are in ruins with the passage of time exposing cracked walls and fallen ceilings.

The Río Mundo flows through this mysterious town. It flows calmly, full of minnows that give life to the place. A small well-preserved bridge allows people to cross from one side to the other in order to appreciate a picturesque view. Water from a fountain flows incessantly. Sitting by this fountain, listening to the sound of running water, it is easy to remember the past and imagine the inhabitants of yesteryear performing their daily tasks.

IN THE VALL DE GALLINERA, LIES THE SMALL ABANDONED TOWN OF LLOMBAI, with its one street of ruined houses. The town has one restored building which has signs of temporary life, although there has been no permanent population here since the 1970s, when its last inhabitant died.

At the entrance to the town an old oil mill can be seen. Next to the ravine, is a wash house with an old three-jet fountain. Llombai's natural position gives a fabulous panoramic view over the Vall de Gallinera, rich with almond blossoms, olives, and seasonal cherry trees. At one time it was a hub for other villages accessed by ancient tracks radiating out across the Vall de Gallinera through beautiful undulating landscape.

LOCATIONS

Esco, Navarre.
Map reference 42 3707 N, 1 0329 W.
Nearest large town - Pamplona.

Moya, Cuenca.
Map reference 39 5654 N, 1 2204 W.
Nearest large towns - Cuenca or Teruel.

Penarrubia, Andalusia.
Map reference 36 5700 N, 4 500 W.
Nearest large town - Malaga.

Alcadima, Lietor, Albacete.
Map reference 38 3251 N, 2 0213 W.
Nearest large town - Albacete.
Llombai, Valencia Province.
Map reference 39 1721 N, 0 3530 W.
Nearest large town - Valencia

9. BUSOT
preventorio de aguas de Busot

A LONG TIME AGO, THE PREVENTORIO (SANATORIUM) AGUAS DE BUSOT, HOSTED WEALTHY TRAVELLERS WHO wanted to relax and enjoy the benefits from the hot springs of Sierra Cabezon de Oro. Built in the 19th century as the resort of the bourgeoisie, it was originally named Hotel Miramar Estacion de Invierno (meaning, hotel of the winter season).

This complex was created by the Count of Casa de Rojas and Marques de Bosch. The original project consisted of two buildings. One of them was prepared for customers with money. The other was built for the poorest of people.

Within the walls of the luxury hotel, there were not only spa rooms, but luxury facilities such as a casino, a banquet hall, a chapel, and a playground for children. The hotel flourished until 1930, when the owner lost it in a game of poker. In 1936, the Spanish government bought the building in order to open a hospital, primarily for children with tuberculosis. However, the hospital was closed in the middle of the last century. Since then, the building has been abandoned. Today it is in ruins - one of the most interesting, abandoned places in Alicante Province.

What happened to the Preventorio de Aguas de Busot? When tuberculosis was finally eradicated, the building closed. In 1967 it was abandoned. In 2006 it was acquired for restoration. The intention was to build a new spa, a luxury hotel with swimming pools, hot springs, massage, sauna, relaxation rooms, gym, etc. But this project has not yet happened.

To avoid building deterioration the area is surrounded by a metal fence. However, despite attempts to preserve it, vandalism has taken place. Today it cannot be visited since it is private property and access is prohibited. However, it can be approached and seen from a reasonable distance. There are many people who come here, due to an interest aroused by mystery and intrigue hidden in its walls. Most just want to know or investigate if there are any strange presences (such as ghosts).

Local residents tell horror stories about paranormal activities, which attract many ghost hunters. There have been several television programs about paranormal events that have allegedly occurred in the Preventorio de Aguas de Busot; white ladies appearing between walls, children›s voices calling for help, or strange noises. It is not known if it is reality or fantasy, but ghosts seem to be part of the history of this place.

Busot itself is a charming town located inland between Alicante and Benidorm. Its origin dates back to Moorish times and therefore Busot has a rich cultural heritage. It is located between the sea and the mountains, making it a perfect place for hikers. A dominating presence is the Castle of Busot, a Muslim fortress from the 12th century. At that time, it was the border between the kingdoms of Castile and Valencia.

LOCATION

Busot, Alicante Province.
Map reference 38 2855 N, 0 2458 W.
Nearest large town - Alicante.

10. BESALU
a medieval town

GIRONA PROVINCE IS HOME TO WONDERFUL MEDIEVAL PLACES.
The first thing that grabs your attention approaching the large medieval town of Besalu is its magnificent 12th century Romanesque bridge over the Fluvia river. Without a doubt it is the most emblematic of Besalu's features guarding the entrance to the old town. Supported by seven arcs and two towers, the bridge is very well preserved and a fine example of Medieval architecture. It leads visitors into the town, with its arcaded streets, cobblestone alleys and squares. There's a wonderful array of shops selling local produce and handicrafts.

Besalu has a long history being one of the most important towns in Catalonia. There are traces of settlements in the area since Roman times. The name Besalu itself is thought to derive from the Latin 'bisuldunum' meaning 'fort on a mountain between two rivers.' Besalu and other charming medieval places are located in the province of Girona, close to Barcelona. It is surrounded by a variety of green mountains and grasslands.

One of the most notable features of Besalu's history is the important Jewish settlement which once stood here. Like many places in Catalonia, the Jewish community lived in a relatively peaceful coexistence with the local Christian community. There were some massacres carried out against the Jews during the late 14th and early 15th centuries, however, in Besalu there was relatively little bloodshed. It is believed the local Jewish families were allowed to leave the city and flee elsewhere.

Traces of Besalu's Jewish past are still visible. The town is famous for the ritual purification baths known as 'mikveh'. Discovered by chance in 1964, the baths have been dated to the

12th century and are believed to be some of the oldest Jewish baths in Europe. The fact the baths are so well preserved is attributed to the quality of the soil and water which surround the mikveh.

A large section of the original town walls, which date back to the 12th century, still remain intact and contain a number of old gateways leading into town. Inside its walls Besalu is a charming maze of stone walls and cobbled streets which has barely changed since the Middle Ages. The epicentre of the old town is the main square, the Placa de la Llibertat, which is home today to a number of restaurants and artisan shops.

There are four other smaller, but equally attractive medieval villages nearby - Castellfollit de la Roca, Vall d'en Bas, Mieres and Sant Joan les Fonts. Add Girona too.

IT IS CALLED THE DEVIL'S BRIDGE, ANOTHER PART OF THE ROMAN ROAD, THE VIA AUGUSTA, mentioned elsewhere in this book. Close to the cava wineries at Penedes the bridge, which crosses the Llobregat River between Martorell and Castellbisbal in Catalonia, dates from 10 BC and was essential for movement by the Roman Empire. It is hard to believe this pointed bridge carried heavy Roman traffic. In fact, it did not. Despite the genius of Roman builders, the bridge fell, presumably due to flooding. This new incredible pointed shape is credited to a medieval rebuild in 1295. The bridge enjoyed another remake in 1768

only to be destroyed during the Civil War and rebuilt yet again in 1963.

Quite a few bridges or aqueducts in Spain are called 'the devils bridge' but the Point del Diable and its gravity defying structure has a surprising stabilizing device. It just required a little ingenuity. The highest arch has an opening 145 feet high and is quite thin, but the weight of its little chapel-shaped building on top is actually keeping it stable. It also was convenient for taking tolls between the two old towns.

LOCATIONS

Besalu, Catalonia.

Map reference 42 1201 N, 2 4143 W.

Nearest large town - Girona.

Point del Diable, Catalonia.

Map reference 41 2915 N, 1 5607 W.

Nearest large place – Girona or Barcelona.

11. BUY A RUIN
and a village too

FAR AWAY FROM TARMAC, EXHAUST FUMES AND THE STRESS OF CITY LIFE, there is an alternative lifestyle to be had in more than 3,000 deserted villages in Galicia, Castilla y León, Aragón, and Asturias. Although many cannot be sold due to the lack of basic paperwork, hundreds are on the market, seeking a second chance in the shape of a new owner.

In the second half of the 20th century, there was strong emigration from rural life to the city. Spaniards emigrated to seek better living conditions; to get a job and have better healthcare. Nothing new here – it happens the world over, hundreds of villages in rural area gradually depopulating. There are many towns which yesterday were part of history but today are abandoned and in ruins. They deserve an opportunity to be saved.

Demonstrators often march to the Spanish capital calling for better access to infrastructure and services in Spain's dwindling towns and villages. It's a demand for an urgent solution to Spain's problem of depopulation a 'revolt against an empty Spain.' They demand a plan to help them live in dwindling villages and in declining provincial towns.

Politicians have no real answer. It is a simple case of demographics. In Spain, 48% of municipalities have a population density of less than 12.5 inhabitants per square kilometre, a figure the European Union considers to be exceptionally low. Between 2011 and 2017, approximately 62% of towns lost inhabitants, according to government data, and even cities with a population between 20,000 and 50,000 have also been in decline.

Today in Spain, even 26 provincial capitals are losing inhabitants. And if these capitals are declining, imagine what is happening in towns and villages. The haemorrhaging cannot be stopped, equally the revolt of an empty Spain won't be silenced. Where does this lead?

In order to sell ruins or indeed whole villages, specialist estate agencies exist. One such agent has 110 villages on its books already to sell. The average price for a village lies somewhere between €200,000 and €450,000. Restoration of old houses is not excessively expensive; the walls are normally sound and make restoration so much easier. In some cases grants are available from regional government and the European Union.

Abandoned villages are getting this second chance because, after years of languishing in forgotten enclaves, these empty villages are back in demand. Although 70% of purchases come from abroad, tending to be British, Belgian, and French, an increasing number of Spaniards are buying into a holiday home or rural life. Buyers want to set up a tourism business or simply live in the countryside. There are also investors interested in hamlets to renovate and sell on. It is also possible to turn derelict cottages into attractive rural accommodation.

The purchase of an abandoned village has shown itself to be more than just a short-term trend. That is why there are an increasing number of owners, who had previously forgotten their inheritance, are now sorting out their paperwork in order to put abandoned homes or hamlets on the market.

Selling these hamlets is not easy. Agents have to ensure they have the 'right to sell.' And that means lots of paperwork. The more property owners, or more likely their heirs, more paperwork is necessary. First, they have to locate the owners – some are dead, others have moved on. Then they have to reach an agreement. The Agents job involves visiting the public notary, the land registry, and local councils in search of necessary paperwork. In short, the most difficult part of an entire transaction is making the village legally sellable in the first place. Local councils offer a good deal of support. They are keen to see these villages injected with new life and help by providing details of the basic infrastructure and property boundaries.

LOCATION

No recommended location. Search for estate agents in Galicia, Castilla y León, Aragón, and Asturias.

12. CONSUEGRA
picture postcard windmills

IT'S NOT ENTIRLEY CLEAR WHEN THE MAGICAL WINDMILLS OF CONSUEGRA WERE BUILT but it does not matter for they became famous when the novel 'Don Quixote' was published. Today each windmill has a unique name taken from the novel, in which 'Don Quixote de la Mancha' mistakes the towers for giants and picks a fight with them in a particularly memorable scene that coined the term 'tilting at windmills.'

Windmills here were used to grind grain centuries before being 'retired' in the 1980's. Consuegra windmills have since been lovingly restored, beautiful, picturesque, and white. One of them houses a gift shop while another is a small museum. There's even a working windmill. All mills were modelled on a Dutch style of the 16th and 17th centuries, with a cylindrical tower and conical deck where a shaft and its four rectangular blades were housed. The wind caught sails made of canvas and turned wooden shafts with gears attached to flat stones for grinding wheat.

Consuegra is just south of Toledo. Drive up to the ridge. The reward is panoramic view of the brown semi-arid plains of La Mancha, with gentle hills that stretch to the horizon, and occasional white house. Put the romanticism of Don Quixote to one side, in fact forget about him, for this is a magical place in its own right, an icon of Spain, especially at dusk, with music playing in the gift shop.

Along the ridge from the windmills, stop at Consuegra Castle. Originally built by the Arabs, the windmills and castle combine to create a unique and unforgettable picture.

WINDMILLS NEED THE BEST POSSIBLE LOCATION TO UTILISE THEIR WIND POWER SOURCE. Remains can normally be found on high ground near villages, on the coast, or on top of cliffs. Many windmills date from pre-Moor times. Near the coastal town of Javea, there are remains of eleven windmills on a cliff edge. Built in the 18th century these windmills were built in a cylindrical shape, over six metres in diameter and a height of seven metres. Nowadays they are in disuse. Three out of the 11 belong to the City council, the others are private property. All of them are partly restored. Javea is known for its beautiful coves of crystal-clear water, a unique landscape surrounded by nature, cliffs and places of interest such as windmills.

There are 150 windmills, or remains of windmills around Cartagena. Many can be seen from the autovia. Some have been restored to full working order, but others are no more than circles of stones where once wind turned sails. They were used to raise underground water for irrigation.

TODAY A NEW TYPE OF WINDMILL DOTS THE SPANISH LANDSCAPE. Thousands of tall, elegant, graceful, slowly moving, white windmills used for power generation, more than any country in Europe. The amount of energy from Spain's wind powered generators exceeds the amount of energy supplied by its seven nuclear power stations. The capacity of wind power depends on weather conditions. Periods of peak demand, usually when it is either extremely hot or very cold, often coincides with periods of low wind.

LOCATIONS

Consuegra, La Mancha.
Map reference 39 3151 N, 3 4040 W.
Nearest large town - Toledo

Javea, Alicante Province.
Map reference 38 4721 N, 0 0957 W.
Nearest large town - Alicante.

13. CADIZ
watch towers

WATCH TOWERS, TO PROVIDE EARLY WARNING OF PIRATE RAIDS, WERE BUILT IN THE 16th CENTURY along the coast. Raids by ships from Africa were quite common. After the final expulsion of the Moors, raids became so frequent authorities had to take steps to combat them by building towers and providing a fleet of defensive ships. The primary aim of towers were to watch for pirates and to signal an early warning so local inhabitants could go into hiding. The warnings were smoke signals by day and the light of fire at night.

One common feature noticed today is a rough opening at high level. This was the 'door of the tower', which was reached from outside by a rope ladder. Inside this entrance is a room with a domed ceiling and a flight of stairs up to a rooftop terrace. Some towers have an overhang above the door which was for pouring boiling oil onto would be attackers.

Initially barbary pirate raids concentrated on shipping, but later escalated to land raids including capturing young people for their slave trade. In 1636, pirates, after pillaging Calpe, they took nearly all the population back to Algiers. They were released many years later when a ransom was paid.

CADIZ IS BEST KNOWN FOR ITS WINDING AINCIENT STREETS AND GLITTERING BEACHES. This peninsula in southwestern Andalusia is

surrounded by water and a seawall encloses most of the old city offering perfect views of the Atlantic Ocean. But this enchanting city is also known for its watchtowers that punctuate the skyline. They make Cadiz one of the most architecturally fascinating cities on the Iberian Peninsula.

The city's unique access to the sea and its strategic location just west of the Straits of Gibraltar hold the key to why watchtowers have become a symbol of Cadiz. By the 17th century, Cadiz was overflowing with successful merchants. Traders, traveling to and from the West Indies, moved in and out of this important Spanish port on a daily basis with merchants observing their ships whenever they entered harbour. So, over the course of the 17th and 18th centuries, dozens of merchants erected watchtowers on the roofs of their often-lavish homes.

By 1777, the city of Cadiz had 160 watchtowers. Today, 126 remain. The extreme heat of the summer months made the roof patios of Cadiz's buildings a popular place to relax, play games, and fly kites. So, the towers were not only places from which to view the harbour, they were also sites for family recreation and symbols of wealth to those who built them.

LOCATION

Cadiz.
Map reference 36 3138 N, 6 1717 W. Capital of the region

14. FARMING CURIOSITIES
Era, snow cave, and wine press

JUMP INTO A CAR AND GO INLAND! THE BUZZ OF THE COAST DISAPPEARS. Walk in the countryside and be immediately struck by the calmness of everything. Listen to nature, birds singing, strange rustlings in long grass made by some unseen creatures, or simply the sound of a breeze in trees overhead.

Encounter some villages that have hardly changed for centuries, inhabited by families who have always lived there; properties handed down from generation to generation. Their way of life is vastly different to people on the coast. Herdsmen lead their flocks to grazing grounds; farmers gather their crops of olives and almonds. Life is in a time capsule.

Rural Spain is where the history of farming is revealed. Take a 30-kilometre radius from the textile town of Alcoi to find centuries old farming techniques. Eras, flat circular wheat threshing areas. Snow caves to store ice. Immovable stone wine presses. None of these curiosities are easy to find. There are no signposts, no guides, at best only a village name and an ability to ask in Spanish 'where is…'?

LOOK FOR A LARGE OLD FARMHOUSE, THERE WILL ALWAYS BE A WELL, AN OVEN, and a threshing area - known as an era. Threshing and crushing of wheat was achieved by means of a meter-long tapered stone rolled over grain on a flat earthen or stone surface. An era was circular, about 15 metres in diameter with a vertical pole in the centre. A horse was tied to the pole on a 7-metre-long rope pulling the stone around the edge of the era.

Eras are difficult to spot, yet there are hundreds of them. Here is a clue – look for a flat entrance adjacent to a path or road; on the opposite side of a flat circle there will be a vertical drop to assist drainage. Another clue is to look for a well, without water nobody survived - an era will be alongside. The presence of eras signifies people grew wheat before the almond and olive crops of today. To find some easily distinguishable eras check the Chapter on Castel de Castells. Look west over black railings upon entering the village; three eras come immediately into view.

HIGH IN THE MOUNTAINS OF THE COSTA BLANCA SNOW WELLS, CALLED NEVERAS, CAN BE FOUND.

They were built in strategic locations to catch snow as it drifted into dips and hollows. Dug deep into the ground and lined with stone they had a conical roof to ward off sunlight. Stone steps or iron rungs enabled snow workers - pressers and block cutters - to reach the bottom. The size and solid construction of neveras are utterly amazing. Snow was commercially harvested, compacted in the nevera and left until summer when it was then cut into blocks of ice. In the cool of the night the ice was carried down the mountains by mule, donkey and cart to distant villages and towns.

Near the village of Agres, a few kilometres north east of Alcoy, stands the Cava Gran also called Cava de Don Miguel. At an altitude of 1060 metres its huge size, thickness and solidarity gives it the appearance of an old fortress. It is hexagonally constructed on two levels. Nearby are ruins of former snow workers homes. A kilometre away is the much smaller Cava de L'habitacio fashioned into natural rock, the most visited, beautiful, nevera in Spain. It has six upper openings and one lower tunnel opening, all with elegantly constructed gothic arches above the hexagonal exterior.

Nearby Ibi has long been famous for its ice cream. Before the advent of artificial ice machines in the 19th century, local ice cream makers relied on ice made from compacted snow harvested in the neveras. In the middle of Ibi, would you believe on a traffic roundabout, a small round building celebrates the towns history of producing ice and ice cream. It is a replica of ice houses that once dotted the surrounding mountains. The roundabout icehouse also features a replica two-wheeled cart that was used to transport the ice from the mountains into town.

IT IS NECESSARY TO VISIT ALCALA DE LA JOVADA IN THE VALL DE ALCADA NOT FAR FROM ALCOY to find a stone wine press. This typical agricultural town, whose main product is cherry growing, has been granted a prestigious Denomination of Origin. It's a small village with a big history. In the Plaza de la Iglesia is an old Muslim mosque. Throughout the town are remains of Moorish buildings. On the opposite side of the road and downhill is the depopulated Moorish town of Atzuvieta and next to it yet another snow well called the Nevera de Baix.

The wine stone press is located about three kilometres from town. Check at the Tourist Office for the route or simply find a bridge to the north over a mountain river and keep going. However, it is still hard to find. A better bet could be to look at a garden in the nearby town of Orba. It has a wine press, mill stones and nearby several water wells.

A WORD OF WARNING BEFORE GOING INTO THE COUNTRY. If strolling among pine trees in the early months of the year, watch out for the Processionary Caterpillar Moth known in Spain as the Orugas. These moths lay their eggs in white cotton wool like nests in pine trees easily visible from below. On hatching the caterpillars make their way to the ground in a nose to tail chain searching for the next place in their life cycle. Do not touch them, or poke at their nests, or let dogs near them. They cause a nasty rash and give off dust causing respiratory problems for adults. Children can become ill; dogs have been known to die. The traditional natural antidote for the rash is vinegar, although olive oil and lemon juice are also recommended. For a dog; it's a rush to the vet.

The only poisonous snakes found in Spain are vipers. They are quite easy to recognise with a triangular head, brown, yellow in colour, a wavy black line down the spine and dots on the side. They measure 60cm and avoid people. Snakes are highly active in warm weather, especially in the middle of the day and may be found basking on rocks. Be careful when siting down! Do not move rocks, remember snakes live in walls. The bite of a viper needs urgent medical attention.

LOCATIONS

Alcoy, Alicante Province..

Map reference 38 4156 N, 0 2352 W.

Agres, Alicante Province.

Map reference 38 4651 N, 0 3056 W.

Ibi, Alicante Province.

Map reference 38 3757 N, 0 3241 W.

Alcala de la Jovada, Alicante Province.

Map reference 38 4701 N, 0 1507 W.

Agres, Ibi, and Alcala de la Jovada are all close to Alcoy.

15. TENERIFE
abandoned sanatorium, water elevator and antenna

WHAT YOU WON'T FIND IN TOURISM FLYERS IN TENERIFE, just up the hill from the new small white village of Abades, are remains of an aborted early twentieth-century building basking in the bright sun.

Those who come to Abades, on the Tenerife coast of Arico, can see a building crowned with a large cross. The locals call it the hermitage, but many people from Tenerife are unaware that behind this construction there are many more buildings, up to a total of thirty-four. It is an authentic abandoned city, built with rough southern stone whose colour blends into the landscape. It is the old leper colony of Arico and it has, like almost everything on this island, a story to tell.

The strange thing about this ghost town is it sits like a shadow beside a newish property development in Abades. If anything, the ghost town looks more like a real town than the small urbanisation below it, which

has more of the appearance of an out of place housing scheme.

The concept was conceived toward the end of the Spanish Civil War. This part of Tenerife's arid, windswept east coast was considered ideal as a location for housing Spain's lepers at a time when the disease was rampant; there were just under 200 cases on Tenerife alone. At the time it was believed that a quarantined isolation in an arid, temperate climate was the most appropriate solution for this malady.

The idea was for a village colony to be constructed and managed by Franco's military. Everything was almost in place. Then scientists discovered Dapsone, a drug that revolutionised treatment and changed the world for those people suffering from leprosy. The leper colony was no longer needed. Three years into its construction, the Sanatorio de Abona was already obsolete. The project was cancelled, construction frozen, leaving different buildings in various stages of completion. For the next two decades the half-built town lay dormant, occasionally visited by hunters and fishermen.

The Sanatorio de Abona, as it was called, included a crematorium, dormitories, a hospital, and an impressive church. It also contained a dining hall, exam rooms, temporary residential quarters and a recreation area. Patients were to be separated into healthy and sick, and by gender.

Over the years the buildings of the Sanatorio de Abona have seen limited use while slowly decomposing. Paintballers and ravers have taken the liberty of using the grounds. Graffiti artists have had more than a decade to add their contribution. On most days there is no human activity and little movement. A few windows have tattered drapes, pulled outside by the wind and punished for not yet yielding to the elements. The former dormitory rooms have broken beds. Wiring has been pulled out of all buildings long-ago, pilfered for copper.

GORDEJUELA IS ONE THE MOST FAMOUS ABANDONED BUILDINGS IN TENERIFE.

Ruins of this industrial heritage site make it one of the best attractions in the north of the Island. The building is only accessible by foot, running vertically down to various points of interest.

The first steam engine on the island was built here. It was called the Aguas de Gordejuela Elevator. Built in 1903 by the British company Hamilton, the station was intended to pump water to banana growing areas and provide motive power for a flour mill. The Hamilton family, still of great importance in Tenerife, arrived on the island at the beginning of the 18th century. They were growers and exporters of bananas, tomatoes, and potatoes. They also had a shipping company and operated coal ships. The complex was ultimately sold to Fyffes.

Today the five-floor building is in ruins. It lacks a roof, doors, or windows. However it is an iconic location that seems to encourage some people to climb its walls, or to be photographed against an ocean background, despite the risk involved.

TENERIFE OFFERS HIKING TRAILS, HISTORIC VILLAGES, SANDY BEACHES AND THE NATIONAL PARK MONTANA PELADA. The route up Montana Pelada is straight forward. Suddenly a parabolic antenna appears. But not just any antenna. It is huge and abandoned. What was it used for? In December 2008 construction commenced of a thermoelectric solar power plant to produce and store fuel. It failed, meaning an early end for a colossal project which left an indelible memory on the landscape.

This 'super paella pan', which lives up to its nickname, has its own place among many abandoned places in Tenerife.

LOCATIONS

Abona, Tenerife.
Map reference 28 0952 N, 16 3455 W.
Gordejuela, Tenerife,
Map reference 28 2356 N, 16 3509 W.
Montana Pelada, Tenerife.
Map reference 28 3213 N, 16 1044 W.

16. SEGORBE, CASTELLON
abandoned doll factory

THIS BUILDING WAS ORIGINALLY A CONVENT WHICH SOLDIERS OCCUPIED IN THE LATE 1930s. Afterwards it surprisingly became a horse corral. Finally, it was occupied by sculptor and porcelain expert Ramon Ingles and his sister Fina who remarkably converted it into a factory for making dolls. After financial skirmishes with local government the building was vacated. Plans to restore it never came to fruition. In 2011, the building's roof collapsed. Nature is now slowly reclaiming the exposed building's interior.

The vacant building is inconspicuous from the outside; without tall chimneys it doesn't look like a factory. This might be one reason why it has proven less attractive to unwanted visitors. Most of the equipment seems to have been left untouched. Judging from the hundreds of moulds scattered around, as well as many boxes full of valuable dolls limbs and hair.

An eerie silence hangs in the air. It's dark inside the old factory; cool in spite of the heat outside. Hundreds of moulds and casts are stacked against walls, over tables and on shelves, almost attractive in their ramshackle regularity. In contrast, the limbs, heads and bodies, strewn around the dilapidated space are creepy, macabre. Furniture, masks and musical instruments are also to be found. Once inside the main workshop a thousand eyes stare at uninvited intruders.

All in all, dolls such as these, in an abandoned factory are quite Frankenstein in their make-up. Another reason, perhaps, why looking at them can be somewhat unsettling.

LOCATION

Segorbe, Castellon.
Map reference 39 4706 N, 0 2801 W.
Nearest large town - Castellon.

17. ANGELES SUR MER

may they never forget

ANGELES SUR MER IS A TYPICAL FRENCH MEDITERRANEAN RESORT TOWN, with views to Pyrenean foothills, neat streets, trimmed hedges of bougainvillea and carefully mown lawns. Restaurants and beach apartments line the sea front. Decorative palm trees and a promenade give an enjoyable ambience. People pay money to sit on the beach under strong sun with shady umbrellas. Eighty years earlier the same sand had been a prison camp, a squalid and dirty space with barbed-wire fences and open toilets.

General Franco's army completed the occupation of Catalonia on February 10th, 1939, the last stage of the Civil War. Watching the Francoist advance, over 450,000 Spanish republicans fled during the harsh winter across the border to French territory. That massive exile was known as la Retirada (the Retreat).

The first refugees were housed on the beach at Angeles sur Mer. They had no protection from freezing temperatures and biting winds, apart from a few improvised flimsy shacks. Most men slept in holes dug in the sand. There was no water, no sanitation and scarcely any food. According to one of the world's finest photojournalists Robert Capa, 'for sport, mounted and armed French guards beat up dying men. One night in February seventeen died of exposure and were buried where they lay'.

The camp had barbed wire on three sides and guarded by Moroccan and Senegalese troops enrolled in the French army. The sea was on the fourth side. 'Here there was nothing. We drank salt water, the sea was also our toilet, so we got dysentery. We slept together, four or five men in a hole, to keep from freezing. They'd give us one piece of bread for 25 people.'

The gendarmes confiscated most of the refugees' identity papers, so no accurate record was kept of deaths, but historians believe at least 5,000 perished on the Roussillon beaches. About 30,000 of the prisoners already suffered from war wounds that became gangrenous during the retreat. Famished and exhausted, chilled by the Tramontane wind blowing down from the mountains, with no change of clothing and only sewage-polluted sea water to wash in, the prisoners caught typhus, malaria, scabies, scurvy, and lice.

Angeles sur Mer remained the main point of passage for all Spanish refugees entering France. Women, children, and men over the age of 55 were sent north on trains, to be lodged in schools and convents. By late spring the camp was over-crowded. Eventually, there were nine camps to hold the hundreds of thousands of people who had fought to defend a democratically elected government against Franco.

Despite their ill treatment by the French, 60,000 Spanish Republicans joined the French army when the Second World War started seven months later. Did they have any option? Again, they were betrayed, for Marshal Petain's collaborationist Vichy government made an agreement with the Nazis under which Spanish Republicans were handed over to the Gestapo. Thus 20,000 Spaniards were deported to Nazi death camps.

FRANCE TRIES TO MAKE AMENDS FOR ITS TREATMENT OF SPANISH CIVIL WAR REFUGEES. Each year Angeles organises a remembrance march which retraces the route taken over the Pyrenees. Regrettably, the internment of the Spanish Republicans is hardly acknowledged in national France. Time moves on, but history is not forgotten. It's a short distance from the camp's old cemetery to the recent opening of the Exile and Retreat Interpretation and Documentation Centre (CIDER) promoted by Angeles town council. Relatives of exiled people have played a key role here. Thanks to their effort, the memory of Spanish Republican exiles are saved. A third of the Languedoc-Roussillon's present-day population are descendants of these Spanish refugees.

Few go to Angeles sur Mer to imagine dead bodies piled throughout a camp; bodies that fought for freedom, losing both to Fascists, to hypothermia, disease, or despair. Many British and Spanish writers, scholars and relatives have made that journey to stand on that sandy shore, watching waves roll up that beach and to scatter flowers on the surface, where they would be pulled by the current south, back to Spain. The most they can do is to view a plaque, which sits at the north end of the beach.

'In memory of the 100,000 Spanish republicans, interned in the Camp of Argeles, during the Retirada in February 1939. Their disgrace: having fought for defending democracy and the republic against fascism in Spain from 1936 to 1939. Remember them.'

LOCATION

Angeles sur Mer, Pyreenes Orientales, France.
Map reference 42 3248 N. 3 0125 E.
Nearest large town - Perpignan.

18. BELCHITE
war torn and abandoned

THE DAY STARTS WITH A PALE BLUE MERCILESS SKY AND AN ICY COLD WIND. Brown mutilated stones leave a desolate canvas of buildings that no longer exist; truncated walls and tall spires that reach skyward in search of forgiveness. There are few places in Spain that reflect the horrors of war like Belchite, a ghost town full of rubble in which some claim to have heard cries of despair. Saying the word Belchite automatically leads to a memory of the bloodiest battles in the Civil War. What happened in 1937 still causes visible scars seen in this village of 'arrested decay'.

General Walter had participated in the Red Army in 1917, during the Russian Revolution. Twenty years later, he led the 35th Division, which brought together the XV International Brigade, with 80,000 men to take Belchite. He did it in two weeks, with a strategy of rapid attacks, heavy artillery, and fighter aircraft. Belchite was doomed in an apocalypse unleashed.

The battle turned into a street war ending with 5000 dead and more than 8,000 wounded. Some escaped. For those who remained their problems were not over. 'Leftists' and their families were interned in Little Russia, a barracks built to house 'red' families as a concentration camp, or as a prelude to being shot. Belchite's ruins have remained unrestored, a landscape of rubble and ruined buildings, now a memory to future generations of the horrors of war.

Belchite must have been a beautiful town. But there are hardly any traces of its former splendour. A network of desolate streets display the remains of its main assets: the Clock Tower, a Mudejar-style building built in the 15th century, the Convent of San Agustín

and the Church of San Agustín an icon of the town whose ghostly aura is accentuated at dusk. Most obvious is the Arco de la Villa, one of the four gates giving access to the centre, the start of Calle Mayor.

There was no wall around the town. Houses formed a defence that served as a wall. It was useful in the War of the Spanish Succession and to stop the French during the Napoleonic invasion. But one hundred and five T-26 tanks, more than 90 Russian planes, cannons, mortars, and hand grenades were not the guns and lead balls from previous centuries.

Up the hillside, the now renamed Old Belchite shows its soul to the world in a desolate panorama of sunken ceilings where wooden beams look like splintered bones; in brick towers falling in moments after withstanding the passing of centuries; in streets that look like veins clogged with debris. Although scrap metal and remnants of weapons have been removed decades ago, bullet casings and combs (support for machine gun bullets) are still visible. An iron cross remembers the place where the bodies of thousands of fallen fighters were burned. At the entrance to the town, written on a piece of rusty metal attached to a broken wall, a hand painted sign says (translated)

'Old Town of Belchite. You are no longer haunted by zagales, you will no longer hear the songs that our parents sang.'

Instead of reconstruction, Franco's regime decided to create a new town adjacent to the old one, known today as the New Belchite, thus leaving intact the ruins of the previous one. The new town was raised from nothing. Many of the new buildings were built by republican prisoners who lived in a concentration camp whose ruins are also maintained, neither rebuilt nor demolished, but standing as Franco propaganda, either to underline his victory, or to mark the barbarism of the vanquished.

In 1954, in the presence of Franco, the new town was inaugurated, and began to welcome residents who until then had lived in old houses damaged by the war, or in the concentration camp. It was not until 1964, when all residents were relocated, that the old town was gradually stripped of ammunition, scrap metal, planks and wood, plus some stonework for yet more construction in the new town.

LOCATED NEAR ZARAGOZA, MANY PEOPLE VISIT BELCHITE. It is necessary to contact the City Council to book a visit since the area is fenced off. Only small groups are allowed. A night visit is more than recommended since battle information is added to a mystery that comes out of each crack, each fallen stone or each ruin. Old photos and first-person accounts pull minds back to that summer of 1937. The importance of Belchite has served as a stimulus to filmmakers, writer's and to the TV series Abandoned Engineering.

Currently, around 1,500 people reside in the new town. All of them naturally assume a leading role as principals in the memory of Belchite, accepting they and their town will always be associated with destruction and death.

LOCATION

Belchite, Zaragoza.
Map reference 41 1817 N, 0 4516 W.
Nearest large town - Zaragoza

19. CAMPRODON
museum of the Retiro

THE MUSEUM OF THE RETRO IS NOT AN OFFICAL MUSEUM nor does it have any connection with the Town Hall of Camprodon. It is a private exhibition situated in an old garage at the end of Camprodon's main street, opened to the public by Alexandre Cuadrado and Lluís Bassaaganya to show a large quantity of weapons, explosives, ammunition and other equipment, abandoned by the Republican Army and refugees during their flight to France. It allows an understanding of what happened here in that harsh winter of 1939.

The list of exhibits to see is endless: stacks of guns, piles of bullets, ammunition and artillery shells, an old desk with a telephone, an old gramophone, barbed wire, flags, maps of escape routes, paintings, a motorcycle with sidecar and the prize exhibit, a fully restored field officers Studebaker car. A whole day can pass very quickly here. The most poignant exhibit is not a metal object of war but a painting, hung askew in the front window, protected by yellow film, showing war weary refugees carrying their belongings, toiling to the Coll d'Ares in heavy mist.

There have been problems at the Museum. Lately the Civil Guard discovered in the homes of the two museum owners, 37 weapons of war, 10 machine guns, 95 pistols, 30 revolvers, 97 hand grenades, 50 artillery shells and more than 12,000 cartridges. This museum had been visited by thousands of people over the years not knowing that a few metres away, in the basement of a house attached to the exhibition itself, lay a large number of explosives, in danger of igniting, due to degradation.

BEFORE LEAVING CAMPRODON AND ITS CIVIL WAR MEMORIES, it is necessary to visit nearby Baget. Perhaps because of inaccessibility, it goes unnoticed amongst visitors, but during the Civil War it too was on a major escape route. The great charm of this place is its cobblestone streets, stone buildings, fast flowing river, and old-world bridges. There is one good restaurant, with not many alternatives. Its location, next to the first of the two bridges in the town, with the church of Sant Cristofol in the background, is unbeatable. The chef's dishes are a mixture of traditional Catalan food with local products that one would not expect to find in a town lost in the foothills of the Pyrenees. How things have changed from 1939 on this Path of Retreat when it was impossible to buy a slice of bread.

LOCATIONS – both near Girona and close to the Spanish/French border.

Camprodon, Girona.
Map reference 42 1849 N, 2 2154 E.

Baget, Girona.
Map reference 42 1918 N, 2 2852 E.

20. CANFRANC
tales of Nazi gold

IN 1928 CANFRANC INTERNATIONAL STATION WAS THE BIGGEST IN EUROPE and a centrepiece of a railway joining France to Spain. Glamorous and over the top, the Spanish government hoped to attract rich visitors from across the continent to the station's hotel. Nestling in the mountains close to the border it still reeks of Nazi gold with one event which is more familiar to the British than anything else – the filming of *Doctor Zhivago* in the 1960s, when it was one of several Spanish locations standing in for off-limits Russia.

The new Somport road tunnel, located at an average altitude of 1,150 metres, runs alongside the existing railway tunnel, but the France to Canfranc railway line is no longer in operation. The cost of repairing damage caused by a derailment in 1970, on the French side of the 8km-long tunnel, was not something the French government were prepared to finance. The Canfranc rail station continues its slow decadence, looking like a gutted Titanic, its glass and metal innards exposed to extreme elements.

During the early years of World War2 the railway line provided a lifeline for Jews escaping France via the railway station, but by the early 1940s, the Nazis had taken control with a Swastika flag waving above the Art Nouveau station. Ironically after the war, Nazi war criminals slipped through allied hands on these same tracks.

Its rails also transported Nazi gold taken to Canfranc. There is documented evidence of 90 metric tons of gold crossing the border. Part of it was used to buy tungsten in Spain and Portugal with which to armour Nazi tanks, but most made its way to Lisbon and from there to South America.

Canfranc Station is a spectacular building, in a spectacular location, but nowadays it can only be visited on an organised tour. The station is an impressive 241 metres long and inside it's not hard to imagine its grandeur in days gone by. Restoration is under way, but it looks as if it will be some time before it will be returned to its former glory. Try to imagine this place 80 years ago bustling with three floors of officialdom, a ground floor full of passengers shopping before or after a journey or changing money from Francs to Pesetas and back again.

Outside the station, standing on old railway tracks, a rusting locomotive rests, a tribute to rolling stock that plied these very tracks. Seeing abandoned railway artefacts, with the station looming large behind, the heyday of Canfranc railway station does not seem quite as remote. From the tracks the scale of the main hall building with its 365 windows (one for every day of the year) is imposing. Is one of its 156 doors being opened by an imaginary, tearful Omar Sharif?

So, what do you do with an 8km rail tunnel when the only reason for its existence is to be left to ruin? From 1985 the Railway Tunnel now houses the Canfranc Underground Laboratory. Sinister sounding 'dark matter' is being studied here in this remote location. An opportunity and perhaps the best use of an old train station with its entrance beneath the passenger lobby. Secret stuff, like secret Nazi gold.

LOCATION

Canfranc Station, Border of France and Spain.
Map reference 42 4505 N, 0 3052 W.
Nearest towns are Pau in France and Huesca in Spain

21. COLL d'ARES
path of retreat

STANDING ON A SUMMERS DAY, TRULY HUMBLED, WHAT WOULD IT HAVE BEEN LIKE IN THE WINTER OF 1939? Exhausted people, toiling up a steep hill, wearing thread bare clothes, pain etched on their faces, carrying worldly possessions in a sack on their back, escaping the ravages of the Civil War, in hope of a new life in France. There were many 'Cami's of Retirada' in Spain. At least three converged at the Coll d'Ares, a border crossing into France.

Can Planes is an old Spanish farmhouse set in the foothills of the Eastern Pyrenees. A magnifying glass and a large-scale map locate it halfway between Rocabruna and Beget, close to the French/Spanish border. By car try Barcelona, Vic, Ripol, Camprodon and then Rocabruna. It is an extraordinary place accessed by a good forest track of about 1000 metres. The house is surrounded by green meadows and lush forests while the GR-11 walking track snakes out front on its way from the Mediterranean to the Atlantic. This is the route to the Coll.

A visit to the Coll d'Ares on the Spanish/ French border! The first noticeable thing was a cold wind belting over the Coll at such a speed it was impossible to stand upright. A building, obviously an old customs post, now turned into a cafe full of nothing much stood there. Inside there was a line on the floor, one side France and the other Spain, the curt proprietor speaking an appropriate language where a customer stood. Everyone fell for his party trick when standing on the line. 'International'

comes his reply. A necessary laconic smile was the correct thing to do before ordering coffees, tostadas, and croissants in an appropriate language. He smiled wearily.

Outside a sign 'Cami de la Retirada' (Path of Retreat). Alongside an EU notice with a brief description. 'The border crossing of El Coll d'Ares, located between Mollo in Spain and Prats de Mollo in France was one of the most used by Republicans fleeing Spain at the end of the Civil War. It is estimated that between mid-January and mid-March 1939, 100,000 men, women and children crossed the Ares Coll.'

Dressed for cold and wind with anoraks, hats and gloves, history is touched by walking down the Path of Retreat back to Rocabruna then to Can Planes. It's a broad path, sometimes rutted, with wildflowers either side, weaving its way over unkempt green hillsides, through small woods surrounded by rusty barbed wire. The route passes an old chicken shed, an old farmhouse and finally a new building with horses; but little else. This was solitude in the green Pyrenees, on a respectful, silent path full of memory for those who also walked here, some perishing on the way.

ANOTHER DAY, ANOTHER RETURN TO THE COLL TO WALK DOWN ANOTHER REFUGEE PATH to Mollo near Camprodon. This was altogether different terrain. A long hike along the grassy border distinctly marked with barbed wire and grazing sheep. Choose France or Spain from a signpost, then down to Espinavell, leaving behind an isolated expanse of green grass and a feeling of being able to touch the clouds at their lowest point. The thin thread path wound its way down from on high, passing a small river, a valley and two bridges. The narrow and steep alleys of Espinavell remained silent, the natural stone houses folding neatly into the contours of the hillside. Mollo was reached under a blue sky, high hot sun, to be greeted at a bar to cider, black pudding, eggs, and chips. Alas no French celebrity chef worked here.

AND AGAIN, YET ANOTHER RETURN TO THE COLL. This time to walk north, downhill on the Path of Retreat into France, to Pratts de Mollo. The line between quaint and run down can be small. Prats-de-Mollo just about makes it to 'quaint'. It is difficult to imagine this town in winter 80 years ago, full of refuges and French solders – a past erased from memories of hope and despair.

LOCATIONS – all close together near Girona.

Coll d'Ares, Girona.

Map reference 42 2201 N, 2 2724 E.

Mollo, Girona.

Map reference 42 2048 N, 2 2417 W.

Pratts de Mollo, Pyrenees Orientales, France.

Map reference 42 2418 N, 2 2846 E.

22. CONCENTRATION CAMPS
you will be envious of the dead

WHO BUILT THE EBRO RESERVOIRS? WHO REBUILT TOWNS SUCH AS

Belchite, Brunete, Oviedo, and Teruel? Who built airports like Sondica or Labacolla? Who built municipal stadiums in Valladolid and Palencia? Who built prisons in Carabanchel or Cordoba? Answer - republican prisoners sentenced to work as slaves, whose only crime had been to defend a democratically elected government.

Prisoners lived in concentration camps to work on roads, irrigation canals or military fortifications. Forced labour was used to build a resting place for the dictator himself, the Valle de los Caídos, (the Valley of the Fallen), the Bajo Guadalquivir canal, the diocese of Ourese, and the port of Seville. Let us not forget the dams in Tranco de Beas (Jaen), Zorita (Burgos) and Villalcampo

(Zamora), or the Baeza-Utiel railway line and the Madrid-Burgos rail bridge at Bustarviejo. Structures that are all visible today.

Throughout Franco's dictatorship, 296 concentration camps were opened. Some were permanent, others temporary. After closure they were mainly demolished, their existence kept secret for decades. The current generation of Spaniards barely know of their existence. It is almost impossible to find a camp today with sites now the subject of archaeological digs.

Repression was the main pillar of Franco's Spain. There were no gas chambers, but extermination was practiced; captives were exploited as slave labour. There was no Jewish or Gypsy genocide but there was a real ideological holocaust, a solution against all who thought differently to the great dictator. 'We will create concentration camps for the lazy and for criminals, for politicians, for freemasons and Jews, for enemies of the motherland and of justice. No Jew, mason, or rojos (left wing) will remain in this nation; you will be envious of the dead'.

The first camps, created during the summer of 1936, held captured republican soldiers and militants. Construction was largely improvised and in many cases, factories, theatres, schools, shops, and monasteries were used as prisons. Filth and overcrowding were common, so to was torture and abuse. Hunger, cold, and disease were never far away. Humiliation and punishment was aimed to crush the spirit of prisoners, to turn them into submissive individuals, fearful of the dictatorship. Food was scarce, starvation common. A small piece of bread or a few chickpeas to eat during the whole day. Diseases such as typhus, scabies and smallpox were rife. Any attempt to escape was punished by execution.

It all came to a slow, agonising end. Temporary camps were closed between 1940 and 1941, once prisoners had been transferred to more permanent locations. Others were made into work camps where prisoners became 'voluntary' workers. Ten years after the Civil War, 137 work camps were still operative and three concentration camps too, in which more than 30,000 political prisoners were housed. During this period, a concept of a 'penitentiary colony' arrived with 'redemption of penalties for work.' For each day of work a prisoner was deducted two days from their penal sentence. In addition, they received fifty pesetas a day for their expenses.

CAN YOU SEE THE REMAINS OF ANY CONCENTRATION CAMPS TODAY?

Yes, but they are not easy to find. Try looking at a civil war construction project, a labour camp may be nearby. Belchite (see separate Chapter) is a good example. So is Angeles (see separate Chapter). Or try Bustarviejo near Burgos where nearly 1,000 prisoners built a magnificent railway viaduct passing over the Bustarviejo to Cabanillas road (see picture above). The remains of a camp are nearby.

LOCATIONS

Bustarviejo, a railway bridge passing over the Bustarviejo to Cabanillas road.

Map reference for Bustarviejo is 40 5020 N, 3 4324 W.

23. FERROL
faros with a big surprise

THE ROAD FROM FERROL TO THE FARO DE CABO PRIOR IS WINDING AND NARROW. It undulates with woods, bent trees and uncultivated fields alongside. The Lighthouse (faro) soon appears on the horizon set on barren, windy terrain. Near the car park a large blue sign states this is Faro 03220, located at certain latitude and longitude with an elevation of 107 metres. A few metres on, the road leads to a large building with the lighthouse behind. Although guarding 'The Coast of Death' with its flashing light, there is nothing much to see here except the wild Atlantic ocean, white crested waves and the occasional sailboat passing by. Returning to the car park something on the left side catches the eye. Strange buildings not on any map or signpost. Low-lying concrete buildings difficult to spot. What can this be?

Only a few kilometres north, Faro Punta Frouxeria is reached on another headland. Same barren, windy landscape. Same large blue sign. This is Faro 0321, a huge seven storey concrete structure with blue painted edges at an elevation of 75 metres. Over to the right there is a depression in the ground. What is this? In fact, the depression leads to a long dark tunnel with many large rooms off to each side. The tunnel branches to level concrete platforms cut in a vertical cliff face, facing the Atlantic and the Bay of Biscay. Deliberately hidden from the view of a casual visitor, this is a big surprise,.

Both these concrete installations date back to the Second World War. They are Nazi gun emplacements, not for defence as in Normandy, but to attack Allied shipping coming from the Mediterranean Sea into the Bay of Biscay. As Spain was meant to be neutral in WW2 they should not be there! And that's the reason why they are hidden

from view, rubbed out of the history books and deliberately forgotten by the Spanish government.

Make no mistake these are big gun emplacements. Bigger that Normandy. Cabo de Prior gun emplacements sit on both sides of the road, high up on a hill and low down by the sea. The first thing to be found are concrete sentry boxes. Next, large accommodation buildings appear, thin rusty metal frames holding crumbling brick walls. Another block consisting of canteen, communal rooms and game rooms can all be identified. The main gun emplacements, about 10 in total, protrude against the blue skyline. One group of four are together on one level, the others scattered around. With vegetation disguising the outline, getting close is the only way of discovering a bunker. Fixed to the concrete are metal gun turntables. Graffiti is everywhere, a surreal decoration.

There are many other such installations along the coast of Asturias and Galicia, deliberately hidden and difficult to find. An adventurer should aim for a lighthouse, on the NW tip of Spain, on a windy promontory, hidden in undulations or sand dunes. Don't bother with the tourist office.

LOCATIONS – both near Ferrol

Faro de Cabo Prior, Galicia.
Map reference 43 3403 N, 8 1851 W.
Faro Punta Frouxeria, Galicia.
Map reference 43 3705 N, 8 1117 W.

24. TENERIFE
world war 2 bunkers

STRUCTURES FROM THE 2nd WORLD WAR LIE IN MANY STRANGE PLACES. So why are their bunkers in Tenerife? We know that Franco was pro-Hitler, or at least he owed Germany a debt, since the Luftwaffe had been an important ally, not only in dropping bombs but also in providing transport for Franco's initial leap from North Africa to the Spanish mainland. Yet he managed to walk a tightrope from 1939 to 1945, declaring Spain at first non-belligerent and eventually neutral.

Relations between Hitler and Franco were never really close, each making demands of the other which were unacceptable, Reportedly one of Franco's demands was for German aid to fortify the Canary Islands. Given their strategic Atlantic position it was logical (in Franco's mind) to assume a potential invasion by Allied Forces, so bunkers were constructed throughout the islands.

Despite President Roosevelt's concerns a possible U-boat refuelling point in the islands might make them a springboard for Atlantic aggression, there was no attack. The bunkers were never required. In reality these coastal defences would never have been much of a deterrent. But the pillboxes and bunkers remain as a reminder of how the history of these island could easily have changed.

The south east coast of Tenerife is a particularly good hunting ground with a few pillboxes around the El Medano area. One near Montana Roja even has a helpful information board. Further along the coast, the area between Guimar and Candelaria, is littered with easy to spot coastal defences many of which are now used by fishermen. In the area known as La Quinta, on the road close to the cliff face, several machine gun nests stand out among the vegetation. Enter their small

passageways to enjoy impressive views from inside. San Andres and its surrounding coastline has been a strategic point for centuries. Again, it is not necessary to look too far to spot former military defences.

Along the north coast, perhaps too rugged for an attack from the sea, there is a gun emplacement high on cliffs at Santa Ursula, a superb vantage point for keeping a watchful eye over the immense expanse of Atlantic which fills the horizon. The Santa Ursula bunker is small since it does not have rooms, only two entrance passageways and two machine gun nests at different levels. The walls are painted; it is full of rubbish. Apart from that, the structure is in perfect condition.

The most surprising examples of Tenerife's pillboxes are around the southern coastal resort areas. Surprising because new urbanisations have grown up around them. It is even possible to lie on the beach in the shade of a wartime bunker. Pillboxes between the holiday resorts of La Caleta and Los Cristianos have been destroyed to make way for a smart new promenade.

Obviously, given their purpose, bunkers are not the most aesthetically pleasing constructions. But for those who have an interest in Tenerife, which stretches just beyond the sea and sand surrounding some of these pillboxes, they are intriguing keys to a quite different time; one which feels in danger of being lost in a landscape of sunbeds. Today old pillboxes provide some interesting photo opportunities at sunrise, act as windbreaks for sunbathers and are a reminder of what might have been, as Spanish, English, Germans and Italians all mingle happily on Tenerife's beaches while their ancestors had contemplated war.

LOCATIONS – many war remains exist on the island but the most prominent are:

El Medano.
Map reference 28 0245 N, 16 3210 W.
La Quinta.
Map reference 28 2541 N, 16 2959 W.
Santa Ursula.
Map reference 28 2528 N, 16 2946 W.
La Caleta.
Map reference 28 0600 N, 16 4517 W.

FROM THE LAND

25. ASTURIAN COAL
strike, fight and then talk

DURING THE PERIOD 1931 TO 1934 SPAIN WAS IN TURMOIL. The King had run away, coalition governments were the order of the day, trade unions and dissident groups were all scrambling for power. The country was almost ungovernable. Laws were made and the same laws were repealed a few months later. Big landowners wanted more. Working classes became poorer and poorer until, led by trade unions, they revolted all over Spain.

The largest uprising took place in Asturias led by its miners. They were organized, had dynamite and already had workers' committees to direct their activities. Their intention was to stop an apparent takeover by the government in Madrid with a full-scale working-class revolution. Within three days much of the province was in the hands of the miners. Each town and village had its revolutionary committee who were responsible for feeding and the security of its inhabitants.

The government in Madrid found itself confronting a major civil uprising. They appointed Generals Goded and Franco to act as Joint Chiefs of Staff to suppress the rebellion and accepted their advice to send for the Foreign Legion. The legionaries were immediately successful. Accompanied by some Moorish regular soldiers and government aircraft, they swiftly 'liberated' Oviedo and Gijon. Troops were unleashed on defenceless mining villages leaving a trail of murder, rape and torture. After 15 days the miners surrendered.

Two years later, the same again! Franco, Moorish soldiers, Asturian miners and the 1936-1939 civil war. This time the miners were on the government side, but it mattered not.

WIND ON THE CLOCK 70 YEARS. Coal is on the way out, dying a slow death and its death throes have been especially violent in Spain where a struggling industry has long been supported by state subsidies. When the government implemented heavy reductions in subsidies in 2012,

miners responded in typical fashion by holding strikes, sit-ins blockading roads, highways and railroad lines.

High extraction costs had led to the gradual closure of Asturian coal mines. Then under an E.U. ruling all subsidies had to stop. Miners dressed in overalls and white helmets, their faces smeared with coal dust, poured out of mines after their last shift, accepting the inevitable. The Spanish government announced in 2016 a 2.13-billion-euro plan, to ease the closure of its uncompetitive coal mines. The industry employed around 100,000 people in the 1940's which has now dwindled to almost nothing.

TAKE A TRIPALONG THE MOTORWAYS OF ASTURIAS TODAY AND YOU WILL SEE winding wheels that lowered cages down into pits. The unique architecture of mining neighbourhoods pass by; dilapidated factories, old gas tanks and lofty chimneys are silhouetted against a cloudy sky. Be surprised at the harshness of the mining town of Bustiello, or the pitheads at Mosquitera, Candin and San Fernando.

Gijon's former railway station, Estacion del Norte, now houses the 'Railway Museum of Asturias' which tells a railway history that became the backbone of Asturian life in the mining age. Some of the museums steam locomotives come from the Ferrocarril de Langreo railway line

which connected the mines of Langreo to the port of Gijon.

For total immersion in mining, visit the 'Museum of Mining and Industry of Asturias' located in the town of El Entrego near Gijon. Designed to hold a historical memory of mining for posterity, this museum comprises different areas of mining activities; machinery, minerals, literature and everything related to an industrial sociology of mine working, such as the infirmary and bath houses. Put on a helmet and descend into the mine, an underground reproduction built 600 metres below ground. It is accessed through a cage elevator. And once down, a thousand metres of walk awaits, through galleries and workshops, with the roar of controlled explosions playing in the background. It is even possible to ride on one of those little trains the miners used to transport coal.

LOCATIONS – all close to the capital of Asturias – Oviedo
Bustiello.
Map reference 43 2040 N, 6 3146 W.
Gijon.
Map reference 43 3258 N, 5 3940 W.
El Entrego.
Map reference 43 1713 N, 5 3814 W.

26. LA MANCHA
lavender

LA MANCHA HAS GREAT CLIMATIC VARIATION, EXTREMELY HOT IN SUMMER, VERY COLD IN WINTER. If travelling by car massive, flat, brown and green fields whizz by. Sunflowers heads permanently turned towards the sun, gently waving wheat and regimented rows of vines, can all be seen on this wide, parched, landscape. Alas no fields of purple lavender are immediately obvious for they are tucked away in hidden places.

When most people imagine rolling fields of fragrant lavender, they are thinking of France. It comes as a surprise to know the same experience is available in Brihuega, just one hour from Madrid. Known as the Spanish Provence, this region offers an amazing 10,000 hectares of lavender fields producing about 10% of the world's lavender.

When is the best month to view? Flowering lavender can be seen during the whole month of July, although better in the second half when flowering is at its peak. The exact time of day to appreciate lavender fields is just before sunset. There are very few people around at that time, mostly taking pictures without disturbing anyone else. Lavender fields are a photographers' paradise, so photogenic that ladies dress up in bright colours such as white or yellow to contrast with the deep purple. There are also many couples who decide to take their wedding photographs in this environment. Be aware of bees! In lavender fields there are lots of bees. They are working to pollinate the flowers and

don't intend to attack people.

The area is known locally as the Jardín de la Alcarria, and every year in July, fields come alive not just with the beauty of lavender, but also with a special open-air concert accompanied by fine dining under bright stars. The Lavender Festival is a spectacle unlike any other. A formal event, a special event, where participants are required to come dressed in white and take a seat among rows of fragrant blooms to hear some of Spain's finest musicians perform at sunset. When the time comes for the concert to begin, the atmosphere is electric. There is almost no sun. The sky turns to an unforgettable light hazy pink. After the concert, attendees enjoy fine local gastronomy under the moon and stars, at midnight.

Preparing for the Festival, villagers adorn their windows, houses, and restaurants with lots of flowers. The streets are decorated with bouquets and ribbons the colour of lavender. The smell of lavender is everywhere. The Festival includes a program of activities, such as guided tours of the fields in bloom, visits to a lavender distillery where the oil is extracted, culinary workshops, markets, and more.

LOCATION

Brihuega, Province of Alcarria, La Mancha.
Map reference 40 4541 N. 2 5204 W.
Nearest large town – Guadalajara.

27. LA MANCHA
saffron

FIESTA DE LA ROSA DEL AZAFRAN CAN BE SEEN SINCE 1969 CLOSE TO THE SMALL TOWN OF CONSUEGRA. Situated on a high plateau in the shadow of Don Quixote's windmills and blanketed in soft purple crocus flowers, this colourful festival kicks-off the region's harvest season. A festival dedicated to all things saffron.

Festival goers can look forward to three days of activities, including musical acts, dancing in a flurry of traditional costume. As a fanfare there are cooking contests featuring saffron, and vendors serving local dishes prepared with the prized ingredient. The festivities culminate with a contest, where participants compete with each other, to see who can remove the most saffron threads from crocus flowers.

IT IS NEARLT 11 O'CLOCK. THE SUN SHINES BRIGHT FROM A CLEAR BLUE SKY. A purple glimmer lies over the crocus fields. Between precisely planted rows of flowers, local people are helping with the harvest. Stooping men carefully pluck the delicate flowers and place them in a brown wicker basket.

A crocus can grow to a height of 30 cm. 6 petals protect the 3 stigmas inside the flower. It is these 2.5 to 4.5 cm long stigmas that yield saffron. The crocus is sown in August and starts flowering at the end of October. This is when the short harvest season begins. It will end in the middle of November.

With autumnal magic, the fields of La Mancha are transformed overnight into a glorious sea of colour. The time has come at last and the flowers must be harvested immediately. The delicate crocus flowers cannot survive the Spanish sun for long; they risk wilting. To prevent this, harvesters go out every day. Harvesting by hand is a laborious business, but so far there is no machine to do this work 'the flowers are too delicate.' It needs around 250,000 flowers to produce a kilo of saffron, and that's a lot of labour.

From the field, the crocus is taken for further processing – not to a factory but to a house close to the fields. Inside the intense smell of saffron overrides any other sensation. In the middle of the room is a long table covered with a white cloth, on which hundreds of crocus flowers are spread. Around 25 women, most of them past retirement age, are removing the three delicate red stigmas from the flowers. Petals land on the floor. Purple petals may be beautiful, but there is no further use for them.

There is a cheerful, almost family atmosphere among the women. 'That is what it's all about for them, they use the harvest as a pastime, to meet other villagers and swap news. They receive 'red gold' as payment instead of money. They can take a third of their day's output home with them.'

While most of the women are at the table busily removing the stigmas, another woman is roasting them. The aroma is not released until the stigmas are roasted over charcoal in a cylindrical sieve. Some say that saffron can have up to 150 different flavours: it starts sweet, with a slight hint of vanilla or caramel, but over the years, it becomes more and more powerful, like liquorice.

The last stage is packaging. Saffron is rolled into small pieces of parchment to make it easier to fill the one gram and two-gram jars. Once the jars are labelled, the saffron is ready to be sold.

The day is drawing to a close. It's time to go home after hours of work. New blossoms will appear overnight. In the morning it will be time to start again: picking, removing stigmas, roasting and packing. Soon the season will end.

LA MANCHA IS ONE OF THE FEW SAFFRON PRODUCTION AREAS IN EUROPE - the only one in Spain with an EU-backed certificate of authenticity called Denominacion de Origen Protegida (DOP). Though saffron crocuses grow in Italy, Iran, India, and beyond, many chefs consider La Mancha saffron to be 'the gold standard.'

Producing saffron requires lots of labour, the main reason why this spice is by far and away the world's priciest food by weight. Well, is it? The wholesale price of saffron ranges from around 1000€ to 5000€ per kilogram - obviously, a huge variation with price dependant on quality. The nice thing about saffron is even though it's extremely expensive by weight, when you think about it in terms of cost per food serving, it is actually quite affordable.

LOCATION

Azafran, La Mancha.
Map reference 39 2543 N, 3 2729 W.
Nearest town Consuegra.
Nearest large town - Toledo

28. LA MANGA
brown sea over the fairway

THE LA MANGA CLUB HAS ALWAYS BEEN SYNONYMOUS WITH GOLF. Its prestigious courses offer a challenge to golfers of all level. These courses have been carefully designed by Arnold Palmer, Robert Putman, Dave Thomas, and Severiano Ballesteros. Its lush green fairways and manicured greens live and breathe golf. Nearby its prestigious hotel exudes luxury. Yet, sad to say Portman Bay, one of the world's greatest ecological mining disasters lies only a driver and five iron away.

Visiting Portman Bay is like taking a journey through the history of ecological, social and economic disaster. Portman, a coastal town in the Region of Murcia, located at the foot of the Cartagena-La Unión mining Sierra, was one of the largest and busiest ports in the south of Spain. The Romans called it 'Portus Magnus' or 'Great Port'. In times of splendour, it was a beautiful natural bay where huge sail powered vessels docked to collect silver and other metals.

Why was this beautiful bay allowed to become a landfill for mining waste for more than 30 years? The great tragedy began when mining waste began to be dumped into the Mediterranean. Portman Bay became a main point for heavy metal contamination. Dumping at sea was banned in the 1990s, but it was too late for Portman. Here, the blue clear waters of Mediterranean sea are brown, mixed with millions of tons of contaminated debris spread across the seabed.

What can be seen today?

In 1957, the eloquently named Roberto Laundry was installed to clean and separate heavy metals such as lead, silver, pyrites or zinc. During this time the Jose Maestre Tunnel was also built, which served to transport minerals by train. Roberto's laundry, the train line

and the Jose Maestre Tunnel are unused and abandoned in the Sierra de la Union. These facilities are worth visiting for the curious landscape left. The entrance to the abandoned Jose Maestre Tunnel is practically covered by vegetation, making it a challenging visit for the adventurous.

LOCATIONS – both close to Cartagena.

La Manga Golf, Murcia.
Map reference 37 3616 N, 0 4810 W.

Portman Bay, Murcia.
Map reference 37 3500 N, 0 5054 W.

29. MINES
hues of dusty pink, brown, yellow, red & grey

THE RIO TINTO MINING PARK OFFERS A JOURNEY ON A 19th CENTURY TRAIN crossing incredible landscapes, a river with unique coloured water, and a territory showing traces of 5,000 years of mining activity. It has a museum full of cultural heritage, a house that goes back to Victorian England; even a walk on Mars without leaving Earth. Walls of terraced rock, streaked with unusual colours of mineral ores, create an impression of gargantuan proportions that could easily be mistaken for a set of Star Wars.

Arising out of the midst of surrounding greenery, near Huelva in southern Spain, the giant opencast mine of Rio Tinto creates a surreal landscape. Removal of layer upon layer of soil and rock, in the search for iron ore, copper, silver and a host of other minerals, has tinted this part Spain in hues of dusty pink, brown, yellow, red and grey. The depression excavated is a man-made crater measuring several kilometres across.

Rio Tinto is more than an isolated cavity on the earth's surface. Its growth has consumed not only mountains and valleys but even entire villages, whose population had to be resettled in specially built towns nearby. The predominant ores are ferrous, which oxidise when coming into contact with air, colouring land and river alike in shades of reddish brown.

The mines were bought at auction in 1873 by a British syndicate who launched the Rio Tinto Company. The company's British managers soon had the mine running at full steam by constructing a railway to the coast to export the ore. They also built Bella Vista, a purpose-built village for British employees. Known as the 'colonia inglesa', the British style houses, neatly trimmed gardens, tennis lawns, football and social club of Bella Vista can still be visited today. Several kilometres away is the modern town of Minas de Rio Tinto, built to replace an older settlement swallowed up by the mine's expansion. The towns hospital now houses an impressive museum.

Did you know this place was chosen by NASA and the European Space Agency for some of their experiments? All because the Rio Tinto mining basin has a certain resemblance to Mars.

THE ABANDONED MINES OF MAZARRON TAKE US BACK TO ANOTHER TIME. Landscape, formed by mining spoil, tinged with multiple colours, transports us to another canvas. This photogenic scene consists of abandoned and ruined buildings that amaze.

Mazarron is a coastal resort located in the south of Murcia Region. It is characterized by having a great wealth of minerals, such as Zinc, Lead, Alum and Silver. This territory has been used since ancient times due to its proximity to the coast, which facilitated the export of minerals by sea. The industry was developed by successive generations reaching a peak in the 1840s when mining fever was at its height. It continued until the 1950s when the area was abandoned. Currently, Mazarron's mining activity has disappeared, but it's remains can still be seen.

Heading out of Mazarron on foot, the ruined mining settlement of San Cristobal can be reached by a set of crumbling steps. There are lots of buildings to explore and a magnificent pit head. It's not difficult to imagine a bustling community of mine workers. The other mine of Los Perules is like stepping into a psychedelic alien landscape. If preceded by rain the colours are intensified. Visitors must be incredibly careful with holes and cavities along the way. Mining in Mazarron was mainly underground so wells and galleries with depths of up to 500 metres were created. Stick to the paths.

LOCATIONS

Rio Tinto, Huelva Province.
Map reference 37 4211 N, 6 3609 W.
Nearest large town – Huelva.
Mazarron, Murcia.
Map reference 37 3550 N, 1 1856 W.
Nearest large town – Cartagena.

30. SALT
in lake and mountain

SALT WAS A MORE VALUABLE COMMODITY IN THE PAST THAN NOW. Several wars have been fought over the control of salt. India's fight for independence from British rule started over a salt tax. Prior to industrialization, salt was extremely expensive to harvest in mass quantities. This made it an extremely valuable commodity.

Things changed in the 20th Century when salt became a cheap everyday product. New deposits opened up and the economics of large-scale production took over. Today's techniques however are basically still the same as centuries before.

TORREVIEJA IS HOME TO THOUSANDS OF HOLIDAY HOMES IN THE SUN. In glossy publicity material it markets itself as a working town, a reference to salt manufacture from its two lakes.

The salt lakes lie along the costal road from Alicante to Torrevieja. Together, they form a nature reserve called Las Salinas de Torrevieja. One lake in particular stands out, its eye-catching pink colour overshadowing its green-tinted neighbour. The road is narrow, just above sea level while the lakes either side are just below sea level. It's not a place to wander too far from the car. How does it work? Why is one lake so pink?

The strange pink colour is caused by pigments of the Halobacterium bacteria which live in extreme salty environments. They are also found in the Dead Sea and the Great Salt Lake. The colour is also caused by an algae called Dunadiella Salina. These two magic ingredients create the lake's bizarre hue, but despite its colour the water is perfectly acceptable, though it can get a bit smelly.

The process starts in June when sea water passes to the green salt lake. At this time, the water contains about 30g of sodium chloride per litre. After evaporation, the salt level rises to about 150g per litre. The brine is then passed to the second Torrevieja lagoon, where salt levels soar to about 300g per litre. As the process of crystallisation takes place, salt starts to solidify at the bottom of the lake. It is collected, taken to the side of the lake and deposited it into large, pyramid mountains. The salt is then split into different classifications or size depending on its final use.

Let's go back to where we stopped the car on the road between the lakes. Flamingos frequent the pink lake, feasting upon algae-filled shrimps that live there giving their feathers a rosy tint almost matching the water. Up to 2,000 can be seen during the breeding season.

MUNTANYA DE SAL FROM A DISTANCE LOOKS LIKE ANY OTHER MOUNTAIN.
But it's completely different from any other peak in Europe. Unlike other outcrops piercing through the rolling landscape, Muntanya de Sal is made of salt. It is the world's only salt mountain located in the village of Cardona.

During its formation in the Pyrenees approximately two million years ago, underground salt layers were pressed, folded and pushed upwards, forming a layer of salt. The top sediment eroded forcing salt to crystallize at the surface. Interestingly, the mountain continues to grow in height, a result of the consistent pressure occurring below ground. It is one of the few places on the planet where salt sits both underground and on the surface.

Salt deposits stretch approximately one-kilometre underground. The complex offers guided tours where visitors are taken through tunnels punctuated with sparkling salt stalactites and stalagmites. In ancient times this mountain was a mountain of money; salt was called 'white gold.'

LOCATIONS
Torrevieja, Alicante Province.
Map reference 37 5905 N, 0 4051 W.
Nearest large town – Alicante,
Muntanya de Sal, Cardona, Catalonia.
Map reference 41 5419 N, 0 4023 E.
Nearest large towns - Manresa or Barcelona.

31. CAPE FINISTERRA
at world's end

IT IS 6.00 PM, HERE IS THE BBC NEWS. IT IS 6.10 PM, HERE IS THE SHIPPING FORECAST. Viking, North Utsire, South Utsire, Forties, Cromarty, Forth, Tyne, Dogger, Fisher, German Bight, Humber, Thames, Dover, Wight, Portland, Plymouth, Sole, Lundy, Fastnet, Irish Sea, Shannon, Rockall, Malin, Hebrides, Bailey, Fair Isle, Faeroes, Southeast Iceland.

HERE IS THE SPANISH FORECAST FOR Biscay, Fitzroy (Fisterra) and Trafalgar. High wind, occasional gales, rain, and fog. The Coast of Death is normally a wild sea battering against high cliffs giving a feeling there is nothing between this remote corner of Europe and the New World but an enormous mass of water.

Arriving in the town of Fisterra first go to the harbour. On some summer days the unusual can happen. Fishing boats come and go on a sea so calm that it is difficult to believe this is the untamed Costa da Morte (Coast of Death). Meander in a labyrinth of streets in this fishing village, pop into one of the many bars, listen to old seadogs telling their tales, enjoy a plateful of razor clams or any variety of local seafood.

Near Cape Fisterra, in 1596, eight years after the Spanish Armada disaster and after several seasons of British looting on the Spanish coast, Felipe II ordered a Second Armada to sail. From Cadiz, Seville, and Lisbon, some 100 galleons sailed north. Along the coast of Fisterra, they suddenly found themselves in the middle of a raging storm causing the wreck of 25 vessels. Another disaster! 1706 crew members drowned in wild waters.

A must for all who visit Cape Fisterra is its extraordinary lighthouse sitting at the westernmost point of the Iberian Peninsula on the coast of Galicia. Built in 1853 it is known world-wide for its importance in navigating around this Coast of Death. The octagonal tower, made of stone, measures 17 metres and its light perched 138 metres above sea level, reaches 30 nautical miles. Filament lamps emit a flash every five seconds. 'The cow of Fisterra' is a foghorn. On days when the coast is covered in fog, it emits a low-pitched sound which can be heard for more than 25 kilometres.

The Fisterre lighthouse is considered one of the most emblematic places in all of Galicia. An emotionally charged experience can be achieved by watching at the sun going down at World's End, a viewpoint close to the lighthouse. Even better is an evening cruise where the captain positions his boat 100 metres from the rocky shore underneath the lighthouse. As the sun slowly sets, with a black silhouette of ship, cliffs, rocks and people's profile; grown men can cry.

LOCATION

Cape Finisterra, Galicia.
Map reference 42 5247 N, 9 1621 W.
Nearest large town – Santiago de Compostela.

32. CORUNA
Hercules lighthouse

IF FISTERRA IS SMALL, THEN CORUNA IS THE OPPOSITE, A BIG VIBRANT COSTAL CITY with plenty culture, history, and seafood gastronomy. It has a big lighthouse too, called Hercules. From climbing inside the world's oldest working lighthouse, to drinking freshly brewed Estrella Galicia cerveca from the nearby brewery, or riding up a glass lift to Mirador San Pedro, this city has a lot going for it.

Unsurprisingly it has a history of warfare. Of course, the British were involved. On Jan. 16, 1809, the British led by Gen. Sir John Moore fought against the French in what became known as the Battle of Coruna. The British lost, its army evacuated to safety sparing the lives of many soldiers. The French held onto the city. In 1898 the economy of the city suffered heavily when Spain lost Cuba and Puerto Rico in the Spanish-American War for it had enjoyed a thriving trade with both of these colonies.

Coruna is known as the 'Glass City' due to its unique architectural style of 'galleries,' enclosed glass balconies built on the side of buildings as protection from the wind. Most date back to the 19th century and feature patterns, colours, and embellishments. The best gallerias can be seen on the harbour front. Coruna is also renowned for its wide range of restaurants and eateries, devoted to the gastronomic pleasure of fish and shellfish freshly landed at its port.

The oldest working lighthouse in the world, the Tower of Hercules, has become a symbol of city life. Built in Roman times, it is now a UNESCO World Heritage Site. Climb to the top for spectacular 360-degree coast and city view. Learn all about it in the visitor centre. Here too, like Fisterra, it is a treasured experience is to see a sunset from the top of the Tower of Hercules. Coruna has been twinned with the Statue of Liberty because of ties between the two communities on both sides of the Atlantic. The Tower is also twinned with the Faro del Morro in Cuba.

On the downside, despite numerous motorways, Coruna has a traffic problem in summer.

LOCATION

Hercules lighthouse, Coruna, Galicia.
Map reference 43 2309 N, 8 2424 W.
Coruna (also known as A Coruna) is the provincial capital of Galicia.

33. FUERTEVENTURA
SS American Star

FUERTEVENTURA, ONLY SEPERATED FROM AFRICA BY A NARROW CORRIDOR, is the second largest of the Canary Islands, with 150 kilometres of white sand beaches, a warm climate, and a constant breeze. In fact, its name translates to 'strong wind' which gives a clue about life here. Wind and waves which bring visitors to enjoy swimming, kiteboarding, windsurfing and getting an all over suntan. However, no one, just no one, expects winds which buffet trees, buildings, and sand for hours on end. Wind which churns up the Atlantic into rollers and surf. It is a wind which can cause a lot of damage!

The steam turbine ship *SS America Star* was built as a passenger vessel in 1939 with its champagne baptism carried out by the former First Lady Eleanor Roosevelt. At 220m long, 28m wide, with a displacement of 35,440 tons, a capacity for 1,202 passengers and a crew of 643, the *American Star* was the largest American passenger ship at that time and was destined to be one of the most iconic ocean liners of the century. There was nothing to predict sixty years later, rust-covered remains still imposing despite everything, would decorate one of the western beaches of Fuerteventura.

The ship was converted into a troop carrier during WW2, then converted back to a luxury liner for Atlantic crossings and passages to Australia. It had a colourful career under many owners and many names, such as *SS Australis, SS Italis, SS Noga* and *SS Alferdoss*. At the Greek port of Piraeus in 1993 the ship was out of service due to poor maintenance. In fact, it was slowly becoming dilapidated. Expensive repairs were necessary. Drydocking in Greece revealed that despite years of neglect, ship's hull was still in remarkably good condition. It could be rescued. A Thai shipping owner did just that for two million dollars. Why - to convert the *SS America Star* into a luxury floating hotel near Bangkok. Small problem – how to get this massive ship from Greece to the Far East. Answer – it would have to be towed. On January 15, 1994, with propellers disassembled and pulled by the Ukrainian tugboat Neftegaz 67, the ship was heading to Bangkok with the intention of stopping at Las Palmas (Gran Canaria). Without knowing a terrible storm awaited them in the waters of these islands.

During the storm off Fuerteventura, the *America Star* broke loose from her tugboat. Six crew members were sent aboard to attach emergency towlines. They were unsuccessful. Two other towboats were called to assist but on 17 January 1994 the crew aboard *America Star* had to be rescued by helicopter. The ship was left to drift. At 6:15 am on 18 January, it ran aground at Playa de Garcey, Fuerteventura. Within 48 hours of grounding the pounding of Atlantic broke the ship in two. It was declared a total loss six months later.

The *America Star* of course deteriorated. The stern broke off and sank in 1996, leaving only the bow section on the sandbar. In 2005 the port side of the bow section collapsed, which caused the liner's remains to assume a much sharper list. The remaining funnel detached and fell into the ocean. A collapse of the port side caused the hull to break up and by October 2006, the wreck had almost completely collapsed. By 2007 the starboard side finally collapsed causing the wreck to fall into the ocean. Over the years, curiosity about this ship has resulted in people getting into dangerous situations. A dozen helicopter rescues have been necessary and three people have died or disappeared, next to or inside the ship.

Today, a small section of the bow as well as the keel of the vessel are still visible at low tide, provided of course one can stand erect in a strong wind. In the course of the last decade hundreds of images have been taken of the decaying *SS America Star*. Taken from the beach, they mainly depict a sharp bow against a clear blue, or dark sky with angry, grey, swirling clouds; a ship that is majestic, notwithstanding red rust, skeletal frames, wind, and Atlantic spray. The ocean will soon claim all of this ship; 35,440 tons turned to rust.

LOCATION

Playa de Garcey. Fuerteventura.
Map reference 28 2029 N, 14 1043 W.
Nearest town - Pajara

34. HIDDEN ISLANDS
no hotels, cycles, or cars

THERE ARE MANY LESSER KNOWN ISLANDS IN SPAIN. ALL OF THEM WITH A UNIQUE FEELING, where solitude, little infrastructure, and impressive maritime landscapes are the norm. For sun worshipers it is not necessary to go to the Costas, Canaries or Balearics.

Islands are always fascinating and mysterious. They are small universes isolated away from the mainland, and that's why they've always developed their own history and culture. Sometimes it is necessary to escape to a place where no one can reach. There are several hidden islands in Spain, spots perfect for a relaxing day. Some remote, some with the odd shop or restaurant, some to stay a few nights.

ISLAS CIES HAS ONE OF SPAIN'S MOST PRISTINE white-sand beaches. This one is in the north west region of Galicia. An hour out to sea from the town of Vigo are the Islas Cíes, a three-island nature reserve with just a handful of year-round inhabitants. There are no hotels, restaurants, or cars in sight - just swooping seabirds, mossy slopes, and lapping waves. Were it not for its bracing Atlantic surf and rugged granite outcroppings, the Islas Cíes could be mistaken for some paradise in the Bahamas, its sands are so blindingly white. These islands combine crescent shaped white sand beaches with cobalt-blue waters, while rugged mountains and wooded areas stand in the background. Though most visitors come

for a day, some stay longer, camping in the dunes. Just be sure to book ahead, as there's a cap on visitor numbers.

ONS IS ANOTHER GALACIAN BEAUTY, A WHITE SAND PARADISE CLOSE TO THE CIE ISLANDS. With five pristine beaches and one tiny village, there's much to savour. Walk for hours on its winding trails across powdery sands. Take a dip in the azure water along the way. One of the trails goes to the Buranco de Inferno, a marine cave that was considered by some legends, to be the entrance to hell. Here you can hear the sound of the ocean or the 'cries of souls that have been punished'. Ons in its heyday was home to a vibrant fishing community of more than 500 people. Today, that number hovers around 70, but a healthy influx of summer day-trippers from mainland Galicia helps the local economy. The island is home to some of the region's top seafood, so try Ons-style octopus, a colourful plate with potatoes dressed in a sauce of onion, garlic and paprika, served steaming on wooden slabs.

THE LOW-LYING ISLAND OF TABARCA, WHERE SEA MEETS THE SKY, IS NOT VISIBLE. In fact, Tabarca means 'flat island'. Located close to Santa Pola near Alicante it's the only inhabited island in this region. The island was an old refuge for Berber pirates who sailed in the Mediterranean from ports in North Africa. In the 17th century they were expelled, and a fortification built which can be visited today. Tabarca is a sun-drenched, windswept, speck in the Mediterranean inhabited year-round by just 50 hardy souls. For just two summer months visitors escape the Costa Blanca, eager to swap soaring hotels for charming low built white houses and medieval walls. It has an arty vibe, some shops and a few delicious restaurants. How to get there – a day trip by boat from Santa Pola or Alicante.

SANCTI PETRI IS A SMALL, VERY HOT ISLAND IN THE ATLANTIC SOUTH OF CADIZ. It was a prosperous place supported by tuna fishing but now has become rubble, moss, and nitrate. On the island is a castle and tower built during the 16th and 17th centuries in order to defend the area from

pirates (similar to Tabarca above). It sits opposite the mainland Port of Sancti Petri, in a strategic location between the Strait of Gibraltar and the mouth of the Guadalquivir River. The sea between Sancti Petri and the Port of Sancti was home to tuna fishing. Tuna on their migration from the Arctic

Circle to the Mediterranean Sea, passed through the gap between Island and mainland and were caught in cleverly placed nets. The port of Santa Petri is an attractive fishing village with adjoining beaches. There are guided tours to enjoy this unique region.

LOCATIONS

Islas Cies, Galicia.
Map reference 42 1256 N, 8 5417 W.
Nearest large town - Vigo

Isla Ons, Galicia.
Map reference 42 2253 N, 8 5618 W.
Nearest town - Pontevedra.

Tabarca, Alicante Province.
Map reference 38 0953 N, 0 2829 W.
Nearest town - Santa Polo

Island Santa Petri, Cadiz Province.
Map reference 37 2243 N, 6 1312 W.
Nearest large town - Cadiz.

35. LAGUNAS DE RUIDERA

don quixote too

THE LAGUNAS DE RUIDERA ARE ONE OF THE MOST SIGNIFICANT LAGOON COMPLEXES IN EUROPE. Geological formations form numerous depressions along the valley enabling water to flow naturally from one to the other, forming connected lagoons. Fifteen large basins and a reservoir generate an enormous ecosystem over 25 kilometres in length. Set between the provinces of Ciudad Real and Albacete, they are formed by the waters of the Guadiana Viejo and the valley of Pinilla River.

Not many people know about the Ruidera Lagoons. It's mainly residents from Madrid wishing to escape the heat of the capital city, who come here for the weekend. Midweek is quite empty. The most attractive feature of Ruidera is water set in a landscape of great beauty, although in some cases it has been altered by the hand of man.

The town of Ruidera is situated between Albacete and Manzanares. Nearby are some remains of an old Gunpowder Factory built in 1842. The main bridge in town is still preserved, but almost unrecognizable are remains of mills. The Laguna del Rey is located next to Ruidera having small beaches to enjoy a dip during hot days. It is the deepest in the entire lagoon complex, making it one of the best for water sports.

The fortress and reservoir of Penarroya is but a few kilometres away, a point where all the flowing water from the Lagunas de Ruidera is contained. The Penarroya Reservoir dazzles with a fascinating water colour overlooked by slender towers of a fortress. The Penarroya fortress was originally a Muslim fort, passing into Christian hands at the end of the 12th century. A modern slender bridge over the reservoir is closed, however as compensation, almost to the point of absurdity, a man sits in the entrance of the fortress, in an alcove, selling ice cream and soft drinks.

DON QUIXOTE ROAMED AROUND HERE, SHOP WINDOWS IN RUIDERA ARE TESTIMONY TO THAT.
Written between 1605 and 1615, Don Quixote, also known as The Ingenious Gentleman Don Quixote of La Mancha, is a novel by Miguel de Cervantes Saavedra. It is about a wannabe knight, Alonso Quixano, who drags a farmer, Sancho Panza, along on a series of adventures to restore the idea of chivalry back to its former glory.

Miguel de Cervantes Saavedra did not just write about adventures; he had many of his own. He was a member of the Spanish Navy Infantry until he was captured. He was only saved when his captors ransomed him; his family paid for his release. Cervantes also worked as a tax collector, a job which eventually resulted in jail time due to accounting errors. Cervantes's fortune changed for the good after his literary success with Don Quixote.

400 years later, there is a Ruta de Don Quixote, something that manages to confuse reality with fiction, dreams, and fancifulness. A car and imagination are required. Fights against giants that are actually windmills, chasing the love of Dulcinea and the taste dishes such as 'duels.' This is not only a literary route, but also a journey through some of the most magical landscapes of La Mancha. It passes through 13 towns and cities, lasts around 7 days starting at Alcala de Henares near Madrid and finishing at Almagro near Ciudad Real. It is the stretch from Ossa de Montiel to Villanueva de los Infantes that is of special interest. Ruidera is close by, giving access to points of specific importance in the adventures of Don Quixote - the magical cave of Montesinos and the ruins of the Castillo de Rochafrida.

Rather than spend an inordinate amount of time chasing a romantic illusion, consider an alternative. Buy a souvenir. A whole industry is devoted to Don Quixote T-shirts, posters, artifacts, and such like. A metalwork factory in Ruidera churns out the most endearing – black silhouetted sheets of metal, in various shapes and sizes, ready to be pinned to a living room wall, depicting Don Quixote himself, with or without his friend Sancho Panza.

LOCATIONS – both west from Albecete

Ruidera, Ciudad Real.
Map reference 38 5834 N, 2 5304.

Penarroya, Ciudad Real.
Map reference 39 0341 N, 3 0026 W.

36. LANZAROTE UNDERWATER
Museo Atlantico

COMPLETELY SUBMERGED UNDER THE ATLANTIC OCEAN, MUSEO ATLANTICO is a project by British artist Jason de Caires Taylor and aims to create a large artificial reef formed by a set of sculptures made of concrete. The sculptures are located 12m deep and cover an area of 2,500m² on a sandy seabed. It is an accessible place for scuba divers, a magical dive that no underwater expert should miss.

Opened in 2016, the Atlantic Museum of Lanzarote is Europe's first underwater art museum made up of ten underwater installations that offer a reflection of contemporary life. The museum is situated off the coast of the Spanish island of Lanzarote, the easternmost of the Canary Islands.

All the pieces are designed to adapt to marine life and facilitate a copy of species on the island of Lanzarote, since they have been built with materials of neutral pH that respect the environment. The Atlantic Museum represents a call for the preservation, conservation and an education of marine environment and nature.

Designed to generate a large-scale artificial reef it consists of ten different groups of sculptures. There is the Rubicon, a group of 35 human figures walking in front of a wall. The models used for these statues were residents of Lanzarote. You can even see the famous

Lampedusa raft, a reference to refugee disasters. Another component is a group of children in a small metal boat. There are also several hybrid sculptures joining humans and cacti, making a fusion between nature and humanity coexisting in harmony. The sculpture of a couple taking a photo and several photographers, refers to the use of technology in our modern society. Another sculpture looks at a mirror with a reflection of the surface in the ocean.

To visit, a certification to dive 15m is necessary. This can be obtained by taking a basic course of one or two days at one of the official diving centres accredited by the museum.

LOCATION

Atlantic Museum of Lanzarote.
Map reference 28 5203 N, 13 4855 W.
Close to Puerto del Carmen

37. MIXAU
Prestige tanker oil spill

THERE ARE 16 LIGHTHOUSES ALONG THIS SHORT TRECHEROUS COAST FROM FISTERRA TO CORUNA and onward to Ortigueira. A testimony to rocks, water, waves, and wind. In November 2002, they did not help the oil tanker Prestige which split in half, sinking six days after it ran into trouble, spilling more than 50,000 tonnes of crude oil into the Atlantic. At the time, authorities in Spain refused to allow the vessel into a port. As it was dragged back into the Atlantic it broke up, oil washing up on beaches and fishing grounds. Muxia, a small fishing village, was severely affected.

Here, along the stormy Costa da Morta locals are raised with the knowledge that the sea is a capricious neighbour, one that can be as bountiful as it can be dangerous, but no one prepared these people for the man-made disaster that washed up on their shores nearly twenty years ago.

'It was the worst thing I have ever seen,' said a Muxia resident who makes his living harvesting goose barnacles, a valuable local delicacy, off the region's rocky beaches. 'We had a difficult time,' said a pensioner who lives by the harbour in Muxia, a town considered as ground zero during the disaster. 'We couldn't come out here,' said another fisherman

pointing at the beach. 'It was full of black sludge. Wherever you put your feet, you had to wear boots and protection'.

Millions of gallons of oil washed up on shores and in harbours. Locals called it the black tide. It was one of the worst oil spills in modern history. More than 100,000 volunteers travelled to Galicia to help in a clean-up effort that eventually cost billions of euros. According to the World Wildlife Fund, the pollution killed an estimated 250,000 sea birds. The oil spill also ground Galicia's multimillion-euro fishing industry to a halt.

Today, fishermen say their catch is back to pre-Prestige levels. In the wake of the Prestige disaster, Spain and the European Union have taken steps to restrict the movement of older, single-hulled tankers from sailing too close to Spanish territorial waters. But maritime experts warn the threat of another oil spill can never be ruled out.

Now the cry of a seagull is the only thing that breaks the silence in the narrow streets of Muxía. People are resting, the sea is calm. Children swim in the shallow harbour. The air smells of the sea, boats and fishing gear. The disaster is not forgotten. A museum is open daily. Standing next to the pounding surf, above the Nosa Senora da Barca chapel, a large, tall stone obelisk was erected on the hill a monument to the tens of thousands of volunteers who helped during the Prestige oil spill. 'Looking at it now I feel like I survived a war,' one local said, recalling how the fishing cooperative's offices became the headquarters of clean-up operations.

Unfortunately, there was another side to the Prestige disaster – money, compensation, greed. Fishermen from the area, when the fishing fleet was grounded, immediately flocked to town halls to ask if they would receive compensation. Within a week the mayors had the money. 'People even started to sign up women and children as fishermen'. Some received around €6,000 a month. Others in the first month received €2,000 plus €6,000 in compensation. 'We received much more than we would have if we had gone out to sea. It was like a vacation with a fixed salary. We were all happy, to tell you the truth.'

'Many of us lined our pockets from the Prestige oil spill'. A fisherman adds, 'they paid out and paid out very well. The mayors didn't cause any problem. People bought apartments and cars; I am not exaggerating. This is terrible to say, but here, among those who work at sea, you hear people quietly wishing for another Prestige.'

Some people received no compensation from the Galician government when the health department stopped their fish-drying business. They classed it as a cannery and canneries did not receive aid.

Others took advantage of the richness and quantity of seafood found during the oil spill. Only the cockles died, the rest multiplied. 'I was looking for the clean places where the oil spill hadn't reached, and I was taking hundreds of kilos of crabs and octopus. I had no competition. I went out and I found swarms of crabs. One day I took 800 kilos of crabs. I built myself a house. The restaurants bought my catches and they paid very well because there was a shortage. I took them crabs and they would put them in water to see if they released oil. They would smell them, then buy, and say to me bring us more'.

LOCATION

Muxia, Galicia.
Map reference 43 0615 N, 9 1305W.
Nearest large town – Coruna.

MODERN TIMES

38. BARCELONA
fading Olympic stadium

ON THE NIGHT OF JULY 25, 1992, THE LAST RELAY OF THE OLYMPIC TORCH was carried by former basketball player 'Epi' who ran along a human corridor of athletes. Goalkeeper Antonio Rebollo waited. In the midst of absolute silent concentration, he launched an arrow that lit the Olympic flame and made Barcelona known to everyone.

When Barcelona hosted the Olympics 30 years ago it was said to be the 'best in history'. The Olympic dream came accompanied by a profound transformation of the Catalan capital which has lasted to this day. Nearly 10,000 athletes competed at one of the 21 Olympic venues spread across the city. That unforgettable opening ceremony, the gigantic Olympic flag covering thousands of athletes, the rhythm of 'Friends for Life' excited those present and left an indelible memory on the world.

Take a bus, taxi, cable car or funicular railway to Montjuic, one of the green lungs of Barcelona, to a unique small world that houses history, gardens, museums, cultural facilities, and Olympic heritage. The imposing hill faces the old port offering an impressive landscape of the city. Montjuic has witnessed many events in Barcelona beginning with the Universal Exhibition in 1929. But after the Civil War, in which its castle functioned as a prison, the place was depressing. However, with the 1992 Olympic Games regeneration was more than complete; it acquired again a festive and happy ambience.

At the top of Montjuic is the Olympic water sports area with its high diving board. Picture the arched backs of participants photographed, silhouetted, against a clear blue sky. Stand outside the athletics stadium, look at the running track, hear the roar of thousands of people. Most of all,

hear the unforgettable music, *Amigos Para Siempre* (Friends for Life) by Sarah Brightman and Jose Carreras.

I don't have to say a word to you
You seem to know whatever mood I'm going through
Feels as though I've known you forever
You, can look into my eyes and see the way I feel
And how the world is treating me
Maybe I have known you forever
Amigos para siempre means you will always be my friend
Amics per sempre means a love that cannot end
Friends for life not just a summer or a spring
Amigos para siempre

It is difficult to leave the '92 Olympics behind. What do you put in its place? Surprise, surprise, the Olympic athletics stadium became a football stadium. From August 1997 to May 2009, the Real Club Deportivo Espanol played its home games there. Afterwards the Olympics stadium continued to host sporting events. It held the European Athletics Championships in 2010, was the venue for the Junior World Athletics Championship in 2012, and was the scene for the 2013 X Games, (extreme sports Olympics)

Other uses throughout these 30 years have largely been cultural. Concerts featuring world-class artists have been held there. Michael Jackson, Bruce Springsteen, Madonna, ACDC, Rolling Stones, Bon Jovi, Coldplay and U2 are some of the stars that have made their fans happy under a starry sky. It is no disgrace that a slow decline of the Olympic stadium has begun. Facilities are outdated. Memories fade. Only minor sporting activities take place there now, opportunities offered by a stadium to keep its Olympic spirit alive. However, memories and a song will ensure it remains in the hearts of many.

LOCATION
Barcelona.
Map reference 41 2309 N, 2 1023 E.

39. BUILD, BUILD, BUILD
modern ghost towns

THE ABSENCE OF PEOPLE MAKES MODERN GHOST TOWNS A SURREAL ENVIROMENT. It's the scale of these places that are breath-taking. Markings on roads going nowhere. Partly built structures stretching out into the distance. It is easy to visualise how big these developments were intended to be, and how irrational they were in planning.

The financial crisis left scores of abandoned development projects and showed the consequences of speculative urbanization. It was a burst housing bubble, an emptiness replicated in communities around the world, as developers' projects went bust. One of the worst affected cases was Spain, where there are more than 3 million new unoccupied homes in 2020. Half-finished developments dot the landscape

Spain's housing crash was fuelled by a speculative frenzy, combined with loose restrictions and corruption, that allowed plots of farmland near rural villages to be converted to feed a demand for homes that never truly existed. At the height of the boom in 2006, authorities approved 865,561 new home licenses when the economic demand was no greater than 250,000. Quite common were villages of 300 people whose Mayors were undertaking expansions that would double and triple their housing stock. It was more than just one city, town or village, but something pervasive across the entirety of Spain. Large development projects for money was available rather than an actual need.

Banks were handing out loans to developers who had little to lose if a project didn't find a buyer because the money wasn't theirs. Speculative urbanization spread across Spain like wildfire and now many of these pricey and dubiously planned developments struggle to shrug off their reputation as ghost towns.

CIUDAD VALDELUZ IS ONE DRAMATIC EXAMPLE OF SPECULATIVE URBANISATION, close to Guadalajara and about 55 kilometres from the capital city of Madrid. Construction began in 2006. It was intended to hold 30,000 residents, included plans for a train station that would link it to the capital, as well as parks, sports centres and schools. These plans never materialized. Fewer than 3,000 people now live there, without basic services or an easy commute to jobs they were expecting.

Soon Valdeluz became one of the infamous Spanish ghost towns, full of unwanted properties and unfinished buildings. Homeowners defaulted on their mortgage payments, property developers went bankrupt, houses were repossessed, and construction companies awaited in vain for the mass arrival of wealthy upper-class buyers. Today Valdeluz covers just a quarter of the 2004 planned land. In that more compact space, apartments are now starting to sell, rents are going up.

SINCE ITS CONCEPTION SESENA WAS DOOMED. First, the developer bribed local officials to approve this massive project. Then, amazingly the infrastructure for water and gas was not included in the plans rendering completed units uninhabitable. Finally, scant consumer demand and project financing left behind large swaths of empty land criss-crossed up by roads and sidewalks leading nowhere.

Its wide streets are mostly devoid of traffic, that's because most people are working in Madrid. What's more, they park their cars in the garages underneath their apartment blocks. Weekdays is the only time when the streets come alive during school runs.

Surprisingly, the community is quietly coming to life. Couples walking their dogs, children running along wide promenades, people heading to the surprisingly lush Parque de María Audena. Life in Sesena is improving since the development's name became internationally synonymous with 'the Spanish housing bubble ghost town'.

THE BIOCLIMATIC CITY LA ENCINA is on the edge of the village of Bernuy de Porreros, about 10 kilometres from Segovia. It promised to be Spain's first environmentally friendly town, providing solar energy and recycled water for 267 low level homes. A faded billboard speaks of dreams, including communal swimming pools and gardens for residents who would 'live naturally'.

Today, only about a dozen of homes are occupied. One street has finished homes, but half have their windows bricked up to discourage break-ins. On the far side of the development, grass sprouts out of the middle of a street that was never paved. Brightly coloured pipes and cables protrude from the ground. Bags of plaster on pallets have long since hardened.

For the few residents of Bioclimatic City La Encina new neighbours are hard to find. Prices for half-finished chalets have been slashed. Some now sell for as little as 20,000€.

LOCATIONS

Ciudad Valdeluz, Guadalajara.
Map reference 40 3532 N. 3 0634 W.
Nearest town – Guadalajara.

Sesena, Toledo.
Map reference 40 1609 N, 3 4134 W.
Nearest city – Madrid or Toledo.

La Encina, Castile Leon.
Map reference 40 2957 N, 6 3151 W.
Nearest large town – Sergovia.

40. CARTAGENA
looking for submarines

WITH ONE OF THE WORLD'S GREAT HARBOURS CARTAGENA HAS BEEN AN IMPORTANT LOCATION over the ages. Many different peoples have stopped by, including the Vikings, the Visigoths and a few more. It was the Romans who made their mark, so it's no surprise many Roman remains still exist, including an amphitheatre and several ancient roads. Today Cartagena has slightly more than 200,000 people, enough to make it cosmopolitan yet rarely crowded. Cruise ships visit, but not too many. A stylish place where even some of the graffiti is so artistic it can be mistaken for public art. At its centre is of course the Calle Mayor, a ravine like pedestrian street paved with distinctive blue marble tiles. It's a typically Spanish 'paseo' (walk), where families and couples take a stroll together or meet friends.

Of all the marvellous Roman landmarks in Cartagena, the 2,000-year-old theatre is the principal attraction. It was discovered in 1988 beneath the ruins of the Old Cathedral which had been destroyed during shelling in the Civil War. About two thirds of the theatre's building material was on site, making possible an incredibly detailed restoration.

In the museum are fantastic artefacts discovered during excavation. Among them is an altar to Jupiter, a statue of Apollo, inscribed lintels, plaques and Islamic ceramics.

Cartagena is overly blessed with museums. The Marine Archaeology Museum is a place to see remarkable historical artefacts from underwater sites. The Municipal Archaeology Museum contains some of the latest evidence of the Roman settlement from 300 to 700AD, a time of transition to Christianity. The Bateria de Castillitos is an extraordinary mountainous landscape that mixes frivolous architecture with sinister artillery guns. Built in the mid-1930s during the rule of Primo de Rivera, it was part of a series of batteries defending Cartagena's coast.

Cartagena has always had a large military presence. At the Military Museum, a great deal of heritage is held in one place. Cartagena didn't escape destruction during the Civil War. The city was a Republican military stronghold. This made it a target of bombing raids by the Nationalist forces (with help from the Nazis) so shelters were built around the city. One of them now houses the Spanish Civil War Museum

To complete the picture, as with many things in Cartagena, the Romans introduced mining to the area. Close by, Sierra Minera is rich with an assortment of metals including silver, copper, zinc, lead, tin, manganese, and iron. Industrial heritage can be touched at two mining attractions in the area: the La Unión Mining Park and the Las Matildes Mine. The Agrupa Vicenta mine plunges 80 metres beneath the surface. It has huge, nave like spaces and an underwater red lake.

TOWARDS THE SEA FOCUS IS DRAWN TO SPAIN'S OBSESSION WITH THE SUBMARINE, an obsession which started 150 years ago and still

carries on today. Launched in 1888 the 'Peral Submarine' was a triumph of new technology, powered only by electricity. It was equipped with both a periscope for above water viewing, and a search light for crews to view water around them. The Peral was armed with a single torpedo tube. Although this marvel performed admirably, she served only two years, primarily testing its underwater technology.

The Peral was decommissioned in 1890; withdrawn from service, equipment removed, and its hull put in store at a submarine base in Cartagena. It kept moving; but overland. In 1965 the authorities moved the hull to the Plaza de los Heroes de Cavite, apart for temporary stay in Sevilla for Expo92. It was moved again to the Paseo Alfonso XII, in front of Cartagena's port. Over the years exposure to sun and rain took its toll so in 2013 Peral was given a major restoration and finally located to a newly restored annex of the Naval Museum of Cartagena, a dignified 18th century waterside building which showcases memorabilia, weapons, navigational tools and offers a detailed account of sea faring life over the centuries.

Old submarine pens with an immense underground bunkers, were built for Spanish submarines during the Second World War. Work started in 1944; it never finished. Tunnels can be seen from the harbour, two semi-circular holes cut in a vertical rock face.

Building submarines still occurs in Cartagena today – bigger, costlier and subject to intense political scrutiny.

LOCATION

Cartagena, Murcia.
Map reference 37 3734 N, 0 5947 W. Regional capital.

41. CAMPISABALOS

purest air in Europe

THE TINY TOWN OF CAMPISABALOS WITH 68 REGISTERED INHABITANTS, LIES 113 km north of Guadalajara on the flat dry plains of La Mancha and has been declared by the World Health Organization as the town with the purest air in Europe. Its location, away from industrial centres and large cities, at an altitude of 1,400 metres with an incessant wind, is why clean air is now an enviable attraction in this small municipality.

In a nearby field, cows graze with the same sort of calm that emanates from the landscape, where the only thing that breaks the skyline is a group of 50 or so wind turbines. The few people who still live here work mainly as farmers and livestock breeders. There are hardly any cars and the only vehicle in sight can be a tractor passing the church. The noise of the engine blends with the drip of the public fountain and the sound of church bells that ring out at 18.00 hours.

In this small village, wind generally blows from the northwest without crossing any major industrial zone. On a bad day wind can blow from the south. Whatever direction, it is measured from a new point of worship - an air quality monitoring station.

Air pollution occurs when there is a concentration of particulate matter, much of it created by humans. The World Health Organization recommends that fine particulate matter should not be in excess of 10 micrograms per cubic metre as an annual average, and those of larger size should not exceed 20 micrograms per cubic metre. The Campisabalos monitoring station, located on a hilltop 800 metres from the village, shows measurements of 5 and 6, respectively.

It's not just there is no particulate matter in Campisabalos. There's nothing! The only presence on the

streets, which are lined with stone houses, is the wind and the odd dog. No businesses, no stores – just a local nature centre that doubles as a bar. In the entire world, only Muonio in Finland and Norman Wells in Canada enjoy even cleaner air. At the other end of the spectrum, the city of Onitsha, in southeast Nigeria, has pollution that is 30 times the recommended World Health Organization levels.

Locals take pride in their unique situation. Their focal point of expression lies with the Mayor, a retired physicist who used to work as a public employee at the Environment Ministry. He is at the helm of the local council extoling the virtues of Campisabalos.

LOCATION

Campisabalos, Guadalajara.
Map reference 41 1603 N, 3 0840 W.
Nearest town - Soria.

42. GUADIX
one foot in the cave

RUSSET COLOURED CRAGGY HILLS PUNCTUATE THE SKYLINE. Vast desert-like plains are framed by the soaring Sierra Nevada mountain range. Guadix looks like any other small town, with whitewashed townhouses and charming, shaded plazas. Upon closer inspection however, small white chimneys poke out of hills, front doors are cut into rock. This is the Barrio de Cuevas, where much of the town's population live underground. Known as troglodytes, locals have been living in these caves for hundreds of years.

Guadix stands today as one of Europe's oldest settlements, dating back to the Stone Age. The main town, however, was founded by the Romans to mine silver found in the nearby hills. It was later taken by the Moors building the Guadix Alcazaba, a magnificent Moorish fortress nearby. Some of the oldest caves are believed to have been built here during the early period of their rule.

Until a few decades ago, the cave homes of Guadix were seen as houses for the poor, considered inferior to more modern homes. Cave living was associated with poverty, gypsy culture and unclean living due to a lack of modern facilities. Today, however, they are becoming more popular, many local residents transforming these grotto-like dwellings into restaurants, hotels and even holiday rentals.

Cave dwellings are not cramped, damp, cold spaces that at most could serve as protection form the elements until something better could be found. Times have definitely changed. Cave living is now attractive. Guadix has thousands of modern-day cave-dwellers who call these literal holes in the wall their home, some

incredibly beautiful, carved out of mountainous rock, making cave living a viable option.

Once inside a cave house, it is surprising how large and spacious it feels. There is no sense of being underground or cooped up, instead, it feels warm and cosy, sound is softened, unconventional lighting belies established criteria. 'He proudly led me around his home, showing off his various rooms and possessions. The terracotta farm-style kitchen was modern yet rustic, with dried red peppers, onions and garlic hanging from ceilings and walls. He showed me a large dining room, where a long wooden table was covered with bowls of dried fruit and vegetables; the walls were decorated with religious icons and other cultural trinkets.' (BBC/local resident)

It gets extremely hot in Guadix in summer, but troglodytes are protected from the searing heat. Being underground keeps them relatively warm during the cold winters too. Cave dwelling is safe; they are not prone to collapse, fires, or earthquakes. Rounded, whitewashed walls and ceilings give them a light, airy ambience. Number one enemy can be an accumulation of water or excess moisture. A cave that breathes is a healthy one. Ventilation is important, especially with the use of gas appliances. Most cave homes are oriented to take advantage of natural light, often facing south, their layout allowing for natural light to penetrate as much as possible. There is a need to use artificial light too, disguised as a false window, or a specially carved place in the wall.

No two cave houses are the same, which adds to their charm, each with the solidity of earth and silence of a church. All caves are not homes. A church pokes its small white chimney from a round rocky facade. A Cave Interpretation Centre is housed nearby, underground of course.

LOCATION

Gaudix, Granada
Map reference 37 1804 N, 3 0825 W.
Nearest places Baza or Granada.

43. GRANADA
in the hammam

VISITORS ARE DRAWN TO GRANADA WITH THE PROMISE OF A TOUR AROUND THE ALHAMBRA, a Muslim hilltop complex of gardens, palaces and fortifications. That much visited place should not be the only stop in a city that offers so many more delights. With a backdrop of the snow topped mountains of the Sierra Nevada, it's worth spending time discovering this Andalusian city.

Put the Alhambra experience to one side. Let's do something different! Visit El Banuelo the 11th-century public bath complex, dating back to the Moorish occupation. It is also known as an Arabic hammam. There is a cold room, a warm room, and a hot room. It is a rare example of surviving Arab baths restored in the 20th century.

Better still consider the real thing! The whole experience may be mortifying but it's just not possible to visit an Islamic town and not have a hammam. What is the modus operandi you may well ask? Is it normal to wear swimwear? Does it have to be tight 'racing' stuff, or baggy clothes, or nothing at all? Do they smear on black soap? Does the soap go 'everywhere'? Does an attendant do the scrubbing or are you expected to do it yourself? Is the massage a torturous pummelling and pulling, or more of a gentle kneading? Is it man to man and woman to woman? Are there other phases like a sauna? Do they chuck buckets of cold water all over you while lying on a cold stone floor? Is a rest after the ordeal necessary before heading out?

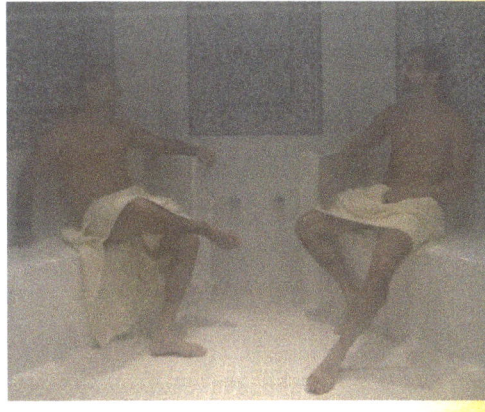

THERE ARE TWO QUITE DIFFERENT TYPES OF HAMMAM. Simply put, one is for tourists and the other is for locals. The tourist ones are more like a spa where someone else washes, scrubs and gives a massage. The local version is almost the opposite, a do it yourself variety.

A basic hammam for locals is certainly not luxury in any sense of the word. In fact, a casual glance at the exterior may even put you off visiting at all. While outside is unassuming, the interior is even less so. It probably has not been renovated since construction. Bare, nondescript shower rooms with undressed stone walls and stained concrete discolouration on the floor.

For a slightly up market authentic hammam, the first stop is the steam room or sauna. The bath attendant arrives, fills up a couple buckets from one of the hot taps lining the wall, then slowly pours it over the client. Then thick black soap to wash the entire body head to toe, followed by more buckets of water to wash away the soap. Next is the scrub. Some sort of exfoliating substance, a bit like sandpaper, is ruthlessly rubbed all over. It's a rough treatment to get rid of dead skin followed by buckets of ice-cold water dumped at head height. And so, to the next room. Its massage time, an amazing deep-tissue sports massage combined with the assisted yoga stretching of a Thai massage. Pounding, pulling and twisting until the customer submits. Despite all the hammam horror stories it is not an uncomfortable experience.

A HAMMAN IN AN OLD MOORISH BATHHOUSE, DIFFERS GREATELY FROM A GRANADA HOTEL SPA where bathing and pampering are a sanitised version of the real thing. There are several hotel spas in Granada, mainly for women to enjoy a hammam: hot and cold-water bath, relaxing massage, aromatherapy, and other treatments. Note the subtle difference here; no pulling or twisting, no sandpaper scrub, no lying on stone floors with buckets of cold water poured over naked bodies – just pampering.

What we have here is a marketing managers dream, an 'Arabian Princess Afternoon.' Entering unrobed from a changing area to the baths, the humid, steamy, comfortable environment is great for unwinding and relaxing. It´s best to go first to the warm bath, then move to hot, and then cold.

Now the real pampering starts. For a 15-minute massage select an aromatic oil from a selection of three oils, Rose, Red Amber and Lavender. With fragrant scent, the sound of water fountains, unwinding is a prerequisite. The old days of bathing, talk, talk, talk and relax, has been replaced by 'strict no talking' to keep a peaceful atmosphere

Many people agree a hammam, no matter if it's the basic original, the one less layer of skin variety, or a perfumed sanitised version, is an overwhelming but ultimately rejuvenating experience.

LOCATION

Granada.
Map reference 37 0950 N, 3 2944 W. Regional Capital

44. MADRID
madness at Atocha station

JIHADIST ATTACKS ON MARCH 11, 2004 CAUSED 193 DEATHS DUE TO EXPLODING BOMBS on four suburban trains their destination all being Atocha station in central Madrid. A few years later a monument was erected to the memory of its victims. The monument is made from 15,100 pieces of glass, each weighing 8.45 kilograms and rising to a height of 11.3m from the ground. The memorial also honours a special forces agent who died when seven suicide bombers blew themselves up on 3 April 2004 during a raid on their apartment.

Hundreds of messages poured in days after the attacks from all over the world. They are now printed on a clear colourless membrane which is inflated by air pressure, rising balloon like inside a tall cylinder of glass.

Access this monument from inside the station. Find a dim room. Then, right in the middle a rounded dome rises oozing light throughout. At night, the cylinder is illuminated by light within its base thus seen throughout the station neighbourhood.

This extraordinary monument is usually visited by relatives of the victims and by travellers to and from Atocha. There are commuters who rush past, people who take a few minutes to observe, while others spend a long time looking and thinking.

THE TERRORIST ATTACKS CONSISTED OF A SERIES OF TEN EXPLOSIONS occurring at the height of the morning rush hour aboard four commuter trains. Thirteen improvised explosive devices were used and all but three detonated. Shortly after the Madrid incident a further attempted bombing took place on the track of the high-speed AVE train on April 2, 2004. It was unsuccessful.

The investigation was swift and brutal. Security forces carried out a controlled explosion of a suspicious package found near the Atocha station and subsequently deactivated two un-detonated devices. A third unexploded device was later found at El Pozo rail station and became the central piece of evidence. It appears the El Pozo bomb failed to detonate because a cell phone alarm used to trigger the bomb was set 12 hours late. On 3 April, following a trace of sim cards used by the bombers, investigators raided a flat in Leganes in the suburb of Madrid. Before any arrests were made the seven men inside blew themselves up. Regrettably one brave special services operator also died.

A video made on March 14th, 2004 was discovered claiming responsibility for the attacks. The video, purporting to be from Al-Qaeda's military spokesman in Europe, said the attacks were revenge for Spain's collaboration with America. Experts at the time said the full extent of the terrorist network involved in the 11 March bombings had to be determined both in Spain and internationally. They were correct, for 16 months later a similar attack took place on the London Underground with equally devastating results.

The monument at Atocha is visible as any city landmark, a poignant, expressive, slightly disturbing memory, to those who died in the hands of terrorists.

WHILE VISITING ATOCHA STATION TAKE A LOOK AT ITS TROPICAL GARDENS. They are housed in the main central nave, a length of 152m and a height of 27m, covered with iron and glass, like an enormous greenhouse. This is a perfect place for tropical plants. The result is a lush garden extending over 4,000m² on the site of the old tracks and platforms, which houses over 7,200 plants of 260 species from five continents. Palm trees, banana trees, coconut trees and breadfruit trees grow under natural light that shines through the translucent glass canopy in near jungle-like conditions. In summer months, when the dry heat of Madrid seeps through the glass roof, hundreds of tiny sprinklers let off a sort of steam, giving the place a genuine look of an outdoor jungle.

LOCATION

Madrid. Map reference 40 2501 N, 3 4224 W. Capital of Spain

45. NEW AIRPORTS
the good, the ugly and the bad

TERUEL AIRPORT SITS ON A COLD, DRY, SPARSELY POPULATED PLAIN IN RURAL SPAIN 1,000m above sea level. A surreal scene greets people speeding along a nearby highway, or in a high-speed train from the Mediterranean to Madrid, as hundreds of aircraft come into view. This is not a typical airport. There are no check-in desks, departure lounges, luggage carousels, coffee shops, taxi stands or shuttle buses. There are no commercial flights here. This airport was built with another purpose in mind. It hosts aircraft from all over the world which have been withdrawn from service, be it temporary or permanent, and caters for their maintenance needs.

It might look like a plane junkyard, but most airplanes are waiting for the chance to fly again. Line after line of enormous jumbo jets appear silhouetted against the horizon. It is not a mirage. It's the largest industrial airport in Europe. Some aging airliners may be scrapped but plenty of new, perfectly serviceable aircraft are in storage. Some are ready to fly but are waiting for financial or legal issues to be sorted out. Some are there because airlines need to temporarily adjust capacity to cope with fluctuating market conditions.

There are few such storage facilities on the planet. There is the Mojave Air and Space Port in the Californian desert, where an arid climate creates an ideal environment for plane storage. Yet another near Pau, in southern France, which has run out of space. So Teruel becomes an obvious alternative.

Some aviation enthusiasts might find it heart breaking to see nearly a hundred or so airliners standing idle, quietly awaiting their fate. Others may relish an unparalleled opportunity for plane-spotting, to capture this unusual spectacle on camera.

WELCOME TO A HIDDEN, ONE BILLION EURO, ABANDONED GHOST AIRPORT. Ciudad Real Central Airport was built in a tiny town, about an hour south of Madrid, in a little travelled stretch of central Spain. It was dubbed the Don Quixote Airport after the literary hero of the region.

Abandoned just four years after it was built in 2008, this modern ghost airport is one of many victims of Spain's economic bust. At the time Europe's economy was booming which meant construction projects were easily funded. Then, the financial crisis hit. Demand waned for both travel and infrastructure investment, leaving some grandiose construction projects abandoned. Ciudad Real Central Airport never reached its planned 10 million travellers a year, not even close. Instead, the airport went bankrupt in 2012 and has stood deserted ever since.

Originally designed to take excess traffic away from Madrid Barajas airport, the airfield is located a staggering 200km south of the city. At a time when low-cost airlines were keeping costs down by serving secondary airports, the remote location of Ciudad Real seemed a little too much for passengers and airlines to accept.

Still racking up costs the airport fell into disrepair, including having to paint large yellow crosses over a crumbling runway so that pilots knew the airfield was abandoned. It was finally put up for sale. The last few years have seen the airport change ownership many times, with an attempt to rebrand it as Madrid Airport South forgotten. An embarrassingly bad investment, the future of this airport remains uncertain.

15th OF SEPTEMBER 2015 WAS THE DAY THE SO CALLED GHOST AIRPORT OF CASTELLON was reborn. The first Ryanair flight came in from London Stansted, approximately 15 minutes before its scheduled touch down at 10.40. There was a crowd to greet it; a combination of ex-pats, Spanish locals, officials from local government, TV teams and journalists who all wanted to be there.

The Ryanair plane was baptised by the local 'bomberos' (fireman). There was excitement in Arrivals as passengers came through. The first couple who entered received enthusiastic applause. Rumour had it, Carlos Fabra himself was in attendance, his 20-tonne statue, and the airport itself, a symbol of his reckless spending.

30 kilometres from Castellon the new airport was one of Spain's private sector airports, one that has so far just avoided becoming an 'aeromuerto' (dead airport), a phrase coined to identify those Spanish airports built as vanity projects, often by a public-private consortium, but failing to attract sufficient traffic to be viable. In this case Castellon had strong competition from Reus airport (to the north), and Valencia airport (to the south), both well-established facilities, connected to the AP-7 motorway.

The Castellon airport project was the personal project of the then President of the Castellon Provincial Government, Carlos Fabra. Construction was completed in 2010 but it too became a symbol of the Spanish financial crisis and the waste it characterised. Before flights commenced, Carlos Fabra was forced to resign from his position as president of the holding company, when a trial commenced accusing him of bribery, influence peddling, and tax crimes.

Despite all obstacles Castellon airport is slowly gaining regular flights from Ryanair and Wizz. It is still far below the figures necessary to make it profitable. A few flights per week, extremely poor airport facilities, quite frankly means Castellon has just about escaped being a ghost airport.

LOCATIONS

Teruel Airport.
Map reference 40 2444 N, 1 1316 W.
Ciudad Airport.
Map reference 39 5202 N, 3 5933 W.
Castellon Airport.
Map reference 40 1218 N, 0 0402 E.

46. OSBORNE BULL
Spain's icon

DOTTED ON HILLSIDES ALONG SPAIN'S MAIN ROADS AND MOTORWAYS ARE MEMORABLE SIGHTS: big black bull silhouettes, horns jutting and cojones visibly dangling. They are painted black, and at one time had the brand *Veteran Brandy* written across the bull in red. Starting out as wooden figures, they were quickly transformed into metal, in order to withstand weather conditions. The bulls stand 14m high born in 1956 as a straightforward advertisement by Osborne Sherry for their *Veteran Brandy*.

A big controversy began when the National Traffic Department, intent on reducing accidents by removing any possible roadside distractions, ordered the bulls to be taken down. There was public outcry across many parts of Spain, especially Andalucía, where the regional government promptly declared the bulls to be part of Andalusian Heritage. The bulls had become such an entrenched part of Spanish culture, the government eventually agreed to keep them, but all advertising had to be eliminated. Now they are simply painted black.

In 2005, the image of the bull was declared a national property by a Spanish judge, after the Osborne Group brought a case against five companies using the bull image on various souvenirs: T-shirts, mugs, stickers and ashtrays. The judge ruled the bull 'has been converted into a national symbol which can be used without the company's permission and is artistic heritage that belongs to the Spanish people'.

The Osborne bull is widely considered an icon of 21st century, its image symbolising an entire nation. It has the same status as the national red and yellow flag. Add a picture of ancient white windmills and you have three symbols that define Spain.

LOCATIONS – all over Spain

47. SOL Y NIEVE
clear blue sky, white snow and big observatory

SOL Y NIEVE MEANS SUN AND SNOW, AN APPROPRIATE NAME FOR AN AMAZING SKI RESORT high in the Sierra Nevada near Granada. Like all ski resorts, the snow season starts in late November, lasting until May. The Andalusian sun has an important influence on snow conditions here. The best time to enjoy fast but grippy slopes is between 9am and 1.30pm when the sun is slowly melting the frozen top layer of snow. After that, not so good.

Even if mother nature does not function, there are 428 modern snow canons to provide its slopes with an artificial variety. A large number of modern chair lifts and gondolas make it easy to reach higher slopes.

Every type of accommodation is available here, large hotels of course, but mainly chalets. Gastronomic services, shopping facilities of all kind, are all easily accessible. After a hard day of sport, sun, and snow in Sierra Nevada, put aside a little energy to enjoy its excellent restaurants, bars and clubs, as they open their doors for a superb nightlife.

However, there is more to this resort than skiing. On a lofty rock, viewing the ski resort and plains of Granada, at an elevation of 2605 metres above sea level, sits the ancient observatory of Mohon del Trigo. It was built in 1902 and equipped with a 32cm reflexive telescope which of course has long since become outdated. The observatory was abandoned. It is a testament to early astronomy, but nonetheless makes a striking image against clear blue sky and white snow.

A new observatory was built nearby in the 1970s, bigger, higher, more modern, and positively bristling with white antenna and even whiter domes. It is directed and maintained by the Andalusian Institute of Astrophysics. The observatory was inaugurated when the facilities of the former Mojon del Trigo observatory became obsolete.

At the last count it had five telescopes, 30cm, 35cm, 60cm, 90cm and 1.5m with meteor detection, photometer, topography, temperature, camera, and radio telescope to complete a battery of analytical instruments. This long-term monitoring programme is to assess the effect of change in the Sierra Nevada region and to gather information to identify the impact of worldwide global change. Such is the complexity and running cost of this observatory it has at various times collaborated with English, French and Chinese research organisations.

With the help of a cable lift skiers can reach the circular radio antenna without difficulty. The actual observatory is a different matter with snow making access virtually impossible. However, during the summer months of July and August, the Observatory opens its doors to the public.

LOCATION

Sol y nieve, Granada.
Map reference 37 0752 N, 3 3714 W.

48. SANLUCAR
solar power tower

A FUTURISTIC LOOKING SOLAR TOWER WAS BUILT NEAR SEVILLA AS PART OF A POWER PROJECT located in the municipality of Sanlucar la Mayor. The top of the 40-storey concrete tower collects sunlight reflected by a field of 624 huge mirrors. The project was widely described as looking like something out of a sci-fi movie. The light is so intense that it illuminates dust and water vapour in the air.

Costing approximately €1,200m, the plant was completed in 2013 and produces approximately 300MW of energy for approximately 180,000 homes, equivalent to the needs of the nearby city of Seville. It will offset emissions of over 600,000 tons of CO^2 into the atmosphere a year over its 25-year life.

This power plant consists of a pair of 'concentrated solar power systems', which function in an unusual way. 624 mirrors on the ground move throughout the day, tracking the sun and focusing its beams onto the tip of a 160-meter-tall tower. The focused light heats up a large tank of water at the tip of the tower, which in turn powers the steam turbine of an electrical generator. This simple process can generate up to 20 megawatts of energy.

Will our future energy look as quirky as a solar power station? Unfortunately, the price of electricity produced by this power station is still three times higher than energy produced by conventional means.

LOCATION

Sanlucar la Mayor, Province of Seville.

Map reference 37 2313 N, 6 1202 W. Nearest large town - Seville

49. SEVILLA
rise and fall of Expo 92

MEANDER THROUGH SEVILLA'S COBBLED STREETS, NARROW ALLEYWAYS AND MEDIVIAL LANES. Linger in romantic hidden plazas, glistening with the warmth of the midday sun and absorb the scent of orange blossoms... wander through the cathedral and up the winding ramps to the top of La Giralda. The sheer immensity of this city is breath-taking.

Sevilla was made famous by its oranges, a bitter sour variety growing on evergreen trees, introduced from Asia during the 12th century. The trees soon became its unique symbol. Now, there are more than 14,000 bitter orange trees lining the streets of Sevilla, an urban landscape providing all round greenery and shade during the hot summer months. Sevilla oranges are predominately exported to the United Kingdom to make marmalade.

In summer it is hot here, ridiculously hot, maximum temperatures routinely above 35 °C in July and August. Sevilla is known as the frying pan of Europe, not a good time to visit its three UNESCO World Heritage Sites. Wait until the sun goes down to join a city of extroverts; open and convivial, with good food, drink, and flamenco.

Shortly after quarter past twelve on April 20, 1992, the King of Spain, Juan Carlos I declared open the Universal Exposition of Sevilla. Known as Expo 92, (along with the Barcelona Olympics) it was Spain's way of showing all it had accomplished in the 80's. Spread across many acres of La Isla de La Cartuja, over one hundred countries were represented, housed in many massive pavilions which opened their doors to a rhythm of ringing bells.

During Expo '92 Sevilla was projected as the sailing point for Columbus and his voyage to the New World. It was also recognised for its numerous spectacular gates and bridges and the diversity of transport within the site; bus, ferry boat, cable car and monorail. An impressive architectural tour of the world ensured countries vied for the most inventive or creative Pavilion. Outstanding amongst these was the Pavilion of Japan the world's largest wooden structure, the Pavilion of Morocco a re-creation of a Moroccan Palace, and the modernistic cube and sphere of the flagship Spanish Pavilion. Other notable themes included the five principal Pavilions - Navigation, Discovery, Nature, Environment, and the Fifteenth Century. The USA were prevented from having the largest pavilion: 'we as hosts intend to have the largest'

Long-term benefits to Sevilla were a new airport, a new river port and a new train station. Not to mention a completely new infrastructure of highways and bridges.

At the end of the Exhibition, various structures were dismantled or demolished. Most, but not all the pavilions were demolished; only 32 of the 102 remain. However, many facilities still stand gathering dust, weeds, and rust. Some have become part of other cities such as the famous monorail which is now at a shopping centre in Zaragoza. Others remaining have been converted into a Science and Technology Park or into a Magical Theme Park.

Still in use today are the Moroccan, Italian, Finnish, French, Russian and Venezuelan pavilions. The Navigation Pavilion functions as a museum. The Pavilion of the Future is the headquarters of the General Archive of Andalusia and houses a large antenna from the

Seville Astrophysical Institute and a life size reproduction of the Ariane 4 rocket, which seems immediately ready to launch a 90's payload.

One current ruin at the Expo is the Mexico Pavilion, where once flowers grew from a bridge, a metaphor of the union between Spain and the Americas. The Cruzcampo Pavilion a property belonging to Heineken, the Discovery Channel with a canal now dry, are both abandoned.

The site of Expo 92 is not just industrial heritage. It is a fascinating mix of new buildings and aging leftover exhibits. For urban explorers it's a kind of modern decay that has a beauty of its own.

Heading back towards the old town of Sevilla, the entire area is a mix of decaying remnants mixed with the new. Walkways, bike paths, and bridges weave among rusting watch towers and dilapidated structures. Unkempt grassy areas with weeds growing through paths are common. The Expo canal is covered with reeds, its characteristic blue lamp posts extinguished or broken.

A sad British ensign, oozing with hurt, the red washed to pink, stands forlorn.

LOCATION

Seville, Andalusia.
Map reference 37 2327 N, 5 5906 W. Regional Capital

50. VALENCA DO MINHO
Portuguese shopping in a French fort

THE VALENCA FORTRESS (NOT TO BE CONFUSED WITH VALENCIA) is also known as the Fortress Valenca do Minho and is only a few metres across the border into northern Portugal from Tui, Spain. It has more than 700 years of history starting in the early 13th century. Throughout the 14th, 15th and 16th centuries, numerous restorations took place. However, it was not until the second half of the 17th century for the already outdated medieval walls to become a gigantic defensive system we can see today.

Consisting of 5 kilometres of walled perimeter, it is an authentic world of military architecture. The project, promoted by the Portuguese crown, was designed on the French model of bastioned fortresses, also known as Vauban. Rather than the square corners of a conventional fort, the Vauban design had an extensive network of bastions connected to each other by ditches and overpasses all designed to improve defence.

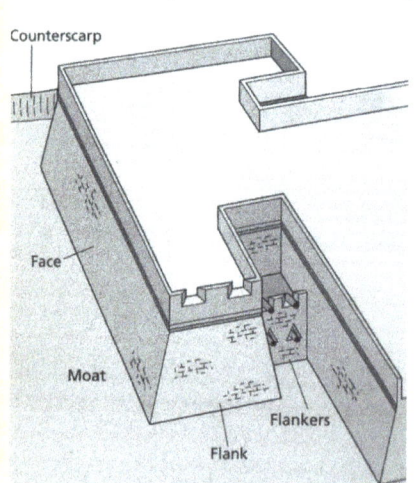

A fully developed bastion consists of two faces and two flanks with fire from the flanks being able to protect walls and adjacent bastions. Valenca's fort is in fact two fortresses, bristling with bastions, watchtowers, massive gateways, and defensive bulwarks.

The Valenca fortress defended a route over the Mino river separating Spain from Portugal. On March 25, 1886, an international bridge over the Mino river was inaugurated, reinforcing the role of Valenca as an important communications hub. The town is divided into two zones: the lower zone is a modern, normal, and an ordinary city; the upper area is an old town within the walls of the fortress.

The fortress has 4 access doors. There are traffic lights to regulate access to the interior by car since the entrance doors are so narrow they only allow one-way traffic. Long queues tend to form, especially on weekends, so it is best to park outside the walled area. Once inside it is a miniature town, with narrow-cobbled streets, churches, shops, stately homes, squares, restaurants, coffee shops and a town hall. The main attraction is a multitude of colourful shops; a typical place to buy lots of

Portuguese textiles, sheets, towels, duvets, and rugs all displayed outside shop fronts. There are clothes, jackets, T-shirts, pyjamas, skirts, tops, some antiques and perfumeries too.

There are several big restaurants within the fortress. Typical good Portuguese gastronomy is a bit expensive but remember there are other options to eat in the new town below. If shopping and eating are off, ramble around a series of exterior walls, descending an atmospheric lane through one of its original gates with a trickling stream running below.

LOCATION

Valenca do Minho, Viana do Castelo, Portugal.
Map reference 42 0137 N, 8 3827 W.
Nearest town – Vigo, Spain

FOOD AND DRINK

51. ASTURIAS
black pudding and eggs

TRADITIONALLY ASTURIANS, AND THEIR NEAR NEIGHBOURS IN CANTABRIA, ARE FARMERS AND SHEPHERDS. Proud people, weather beaten, pragmatic, tough and stoic. It is to the land where they seek a livelihood. Shepherds allow their flocks to roam on beautiful green hillsides, native breeds of cattle graze on sweet pastures, vegetables grow in cool fields. Asturian food, strong and robust, comes from the earth; fabada, smelly cheese, cider, and black pudding.

EVERY NEIGHBOURHOOD BAR OR RESTURANT LAYS CLAIM TO THE BEST FABADA. Great fabadas start with the real-deal 'fabada de la granja'; slender, finger-like white beans of outstanding quality which have been cultivated in Asturias for centuries. Fabada Asturiana is probably one of the most famous Spanish dishes. Buy it in cans everywhere, all grocery shops and supermarkets have it in stock. So popular it is exported it all over the world. Make your own? What you need are beans, chorizo sausage, ham, black pudding and spices.

CABRALES IS A FINE BLUE CHEESE. Its signature taste and blue colour comes from six months maturation in dank mountain caves of eastern Asturias. This cool, dark environment, always humid thanks to dripping stalactites, is a perfect petri dish for penicillin mould that slowly impregnates each wheel of cheese. Produced under a Denomination of Origin, Cabrales cheese is one of the most well-known products of Asturias and is promoted through regional culinary tourism, nationally and internationally.

Cabrales cheese is on the menu at most restaurants. It is available in gourmet food stores and through websites. Better still, it is sold in the local market at Potes, Cantabria (smelt it at 100 paces) and if a cheese taste could be summed up then 'the stinker the better.' Cabrales cheese is so pungent and rich it needs nothing more than an accompanying biscuit to be a satisfying course, only tasting better when accompanied by a glass of sidra.

SIDRA, MADE FROM LOCALLY GROWN APPLES, has been produced here since ancient times and has long been considered the regional 'wine.' It is a low-alcohol drink, slightly effervescent and very refreshing. Cloudy sidra bears little resemblance to the oversweet Strongbow and Magners cider most people are accustomed to drinking.

In old-time sidra bars, bartenders make a show of pouring sidra into a glass from a hight, a technique said to aerate and give it its characteristic fizziness. It also means barmen wear liquid proof aprons or wellie boots as they often miss the glass. There are sidra bars in most big towns in Spain. They bring the taste of Asturias to a city centre in pseudo mountain establishments, decorated in wood, with sidra stained floorboards. The menu? Mainly sidra, cheese and black pudding.

SHOPPING IN A SPANISH SUPERMARKET? One of the first things to notice is a vast and completely bewildering array of sausage – black, red or colours in between, stored in the chill cabinet or dried hanging on a hook. What is the best type to try? Shopping for sausages requires a bit of homework. And the one product with the most varieties is black pudding.

What's so special about Spanish Black Pudding? Morcilla is a Spanish blood sausage which looks like a traditional black pudding. Spain's version of a black pudding is miles away from a Bury breakfast fry up. It's a spiced sausage with a gentle tang and a crumbly texture when cooked. Although the preparation remains the same, it is the flavour and texture that differs from place to place. Different varieties reflect each regions agriculture or history and whether it be local onions or spices that are the extra ingredient.

A most prevalent variety is Morcilla de Burgos. This type of black pudding often includes onion, sweet and spicy paprika, oregano, garlic, and rice. Certain variants do not include rice. A sausage from Northern Spain will be milder. The spiciest in Valencia. And a black pudding in coastal regions of Asturias will have a smoked flavour.

To eat - morcilla is cut into thick slices, which are fried with some olive oil, before being eaten as a tapa or with bread. It can be fried with potatoes, served with poached, scrambled, or fried eggs. And here lies the key point. Go into a small hamlet after a hard day in the mountains, ask the wife of a bar owner for 'the special' and out will come four slices of black pudding, two fried eggs, a plate of chips and a big glass of sidra.

THERE ARE OTHER LESS WELL-KNOWN FOODS IN ASTURIAS. A quick run through the main dishes! Caldereta is a fish stew that contains not just fish, but lobster and crab as well. Add onion, parsley, fresh tomato, a bit of white wine, cognac and it is the most delicious fish stew ever tasted. Merluza a la Sidra is a main course, a blend of hake, clams, onion, garlic, tomato, potatoes, apples, and a bit of cider, cooked in a ceramic dish, then baked.

And a quick run through of the sweets! Rice pudding, the Asturian version is made with rice, butter, sugar, lemon, a cinnamon stick with a layer of caramelized sugar on top. Asturian cheesecake is made with fresh goat cheese decorated with fruit or powdered sugar. Asturias also lays claim to some of the country's most delectable sweets, a case in point, Moscovitas. These chocolate-dipped cookies, have many devotees. Each wafer is covered with toasted Spanish almonds, crunchy toffee, and bitter chocolate.

LOCATION

A central location is Potes in Cantabria.
Map reference 43 0914 N, 4 3725 W.

52. BARCELONA
the etiquette of tapas bars

IN THIS 24-HOUR CITY TAPAS BARS EXIST ON EVERY STREET with tapas culture evolving into a sophisticated culinary movement. Many of the city's top chefs apply their talents to these bite-size titbits. Competition is fierce with adverts for a tapas bar crawl, free tapas and even gourmet tapas. But it is not difficult to find a good tapas bar. At seven to eight o'clock on an evening look for one with a queue outside.

Tapas originated in the 18th century in the southern region of Andalusia as a small snack to accompany a drink of sherry. The name 'tapas' comes from the custom of covering drinks with a plate to avoid pesky bar flies ruining a customer's tipple. Today the three most famous tapas are patatas bravas (fried potato wedges with a spicy tomato sauce), pinchito moruno, (marinated, spiced pork kebabs), and chipirones (mini fried squid).

In a way it's strange to understand the etiquette of tapas. The nature of tapas means that manners and protocol are forgotten in a flurry of sharing, finger-using and general 'digging in'. This is the essence of what tapas are all about. But in spite of this, there is no denying in Barcelona the tapas experience can be difficult to understand..

Tapas is the general name for small dishes of food that are served to be shared. They can vary widely and cover anything from a bowl of almonds or olives to a plate of grilled sardines. On menus you will often see dishes marked with two separate prices - one for tapas and one for raciones. This will simply be  the same dish, but a racione is a bigger portion - ideal for the really hungry. Pinchos is a concept originating from the Basque region of Spain. Pinchos are mouth sized tapas always served on top of a slice of bread. Platos combinados is a name often given to an entire meal on a plate. However, it sometimes also relates to a large plate containing a variety of tapas.

Sometimes on entering a tapas bar the options on offer are displayed in glass cabinets along the bar top. If you go to a Basque style pincho bar the etiquette is slightly different. All of the pinchos are displayed along the bar top. Simply ask a waiter for an empty plate, work your way along the bar and load your plate with pinchos. Whilst eating make sure that you save the small toothpicks that are stuck in each one. This is how the bar staff work out your bill - by counting the number of toothpicks on your plate.

Tapas are not always the chorizo and garlic prawns you might have come to expect. Pan con Tomate is the quintessential Catalan tapa. White bread rubbed with tomato and drizzled in oil and salt, a perfect accompaniment to the rest of your tapas. Anchovies are not normally the very salty type you may be used to. They are served in vinegar with parsley and garlic. Russian Salad is not the healthiest of salads. This is a heavy dish made up of potatoes, peas, hard boiled eggs and other vegetables, covered in mayonnaise

There are no hard and fast rules on what to drink whilst eating tapas. Of course, it may depend on what type of tapas you have ordered. However, you will notice locals tend to opt for lighter accompaniments to their tapas. What you need is a light, refreshing slightly chilled white wine or cider that will clear the palate between dishes, so you can enjoy the variety of flavours experienced during tapas dining.

Locals love to talk about tourists and foreigners who come to the city with no knowledge of its tapas culture. Blow your visitor cover by trying to pay for your drink or tapas whilst ordering. In Barcelona you will be impressed by the abilities of the bar staff and waiters to remember the various orders of hordes of people. Relax and enjoy your food and simply request 'la cuenta'.

The whole notion of tapas is intended to grease the wheels for an evening of chatter, liveliness and camaraderie with friends. All of the dishes will be shared and devoured. And do not, under any circumstances, politely leave the last prawn sitting on the plate for someone else to enjoy - if you don't take it, the waiter will. Enjoy the moment - you are likely to be standing in a crowded space all night - but this is part of the fun.

LOCATION
Barcelona.
Map reference 41 2309 N, 2 1023 E.

53. CAVA
Spain's bubbly

CAVAS ARE PRODUCED ALMOST EXCLUSIVLY IN CATALONIA, specifically in a small town called San Sadurní de Noya located in the Penedes area of Barcelona. Go, have a look, take a tour of the large Codorniu or Freixenet wineries. 'Bottles are taken underground to ferment.' Yes, that's true, well almost true. Large flat fields were deeply excavated a century ago, huge interconnecting brick cellars were then built, soil pushed back on top and green grass sown. The 'underground' cellars are utterly amazing, stacked with thousands upon thousands of cava bottles, all at different stages of fermentation. A visit down these vast century old hidden cellars is a must. How they were built can be seen in photographs.

IS THE NATIONAL DRINK OF SPAIN THE RED WINE OF LA RIOJA, WHITE WINE OF LA MANCHA or the sherries of Jerez de la Frontera? Increasingly it is a glass of cava, Spain's answer to French champagne. Whether white or rosado, dry or sweet, made with native grapes or adopted varieties, a glass of Spanish Cava is now accepted as the one to be raised in 'celebration.'

But let's put it into perspective. Cava has an image problem. There probably isn't anyone who hasn't heard of Cava, Spain's 'cheap and cheerful' bubbly, a mainstay of supermarket aisles worldwide. Ever heard of deluxe Cava – hand-made, artisan sparkling wines of superlative quality with prices to match? Probably not! Cava suffers from an association with the budget-end sparkling wine market. The problem with cava is perception, not quality. The price is so low it gives a poor perception. It is possible to buy a bottle of cava in a local Spanish supermarket for less than two euros. The reason is simple; large cava producers have chased mass markets with low prices.

Producers now believe If you do 'good things' you can have a high price, but if you compete on quantity then you're lost. When margins are so small everyone is squeezed. The product suffers, reflecting in low quality. The way ahead is to go up market. Some producers are distancing themselves from the cava name, arguing the Spanish DO has over-produced cheap fizz, thereby damaging its image. They intend to market their product under a new name 'corpinnat' a product of perfect style and quality, more than a match for any great sparkling wine in the world.

CAVA IS THE CATALAN WORD FOR CELLAR, REFERRING TO A SPANISH SPARKLING WINE protected by a Designation of Origin status and manufactured to a traditional method. This method is virtually the same process used to make French Champagne. The secret of cava is not a place, a grape variety, or the stone cellars in which the wine is matured. It comes from a unique method of making sparkling wine involving a second fermentation within the bottle.

A blend of base wines is put into bottles which are closed with a crown cap or a cork stopper and taken down to the underground cellars. This second fermentation takes place inside the bottle where yeasts convert sugar into alcohol. One of the methods of classifying Cava is based on 'time in bottle'. A most basic category of Cava ages for a minimum of nine months. Cava Reserva, a minimum of fifteen months. Cava Gran Reserva a minimum thirty months and is vintage dated. A new category of Cava de Paraje Calificado must be aged for at least 36 months.

Twisting, and shaking the bottle slightly each day while progressively tilting it downwards moves any sediment towards the cork. Once the bottle is completely upside down, to remove the sediment, the tip of the bottle is dipped into freezing liquid. Pull the crown cap off and a block of frozen sediment is expelled from the pressurized bottle.

A second sugar-based, classification system exists. The driest wine is Brut Nature, which has less than three grams of sugar per litre, followed by Extra Brut, Brut, Extra Seco, Seco, Semi Seco and Dulce, the latter designates wine with more than fifty grams of sugar per litre. Only Brut Nature, Extra Brut and Brut Cava are available as Gran Reserva wines.

Pull out the cork, it should have a four-pointed star on the bottom which, in addition to the label and quality control stamp, indicates the wine is genuine Cava, made in a traditional way.

LOCATION

Penedes, Region of Barcelona, Catalonia.
Map reference 41 2532 N, 1 4718 E.

54. HUELVA
curing the pig

IBERICO PIGS ARE BLACK, WITH LITTLE HAIR AND BLACK HOOVES, which coins the name 'pata negra' which will remain on the ham throughout its curing process, distinguishing it from the cheaper Serrano ham. You will hear it said that Jamon Iberico, is some sort of miracle product. Why? It is low in cholesterol, due to the pigs' acorn diet. It contains the good fats normally found in avocado and olive oil. It is an ecological food as the pig's roam free while feasting on acorns. And finally, it is superb to eat.

Wherever you are in Spain jamon is inescapable. From Madrid's vibrant Museo del Jamon chain of restaurants, where the ceiling is lined with jamons by the dozen, to the capital's upmarket Villa Magna hotel where an Iberico leg is the centrepiece of a breakfast buffet. From the nation's Michelin-starred heights to its raucous tapas bars the hind leg and a sharp knife is a symbol of Spain's gastronomic life.

'Jamon Iberico puro de Bellota' (acorn-fed pure breed Iberico ham) is intensely sweet, floral, earthy, and nutty, with fat so soft it melts in your mouth. Ham that is as good as it gets and the most expensive in the world at 450€ for an 8-kilogramme leg. The cheaper alternative, serrano ham sells at 40€ and upwards in a supermarket. To obtain a high price marketing is necessary. 'A green plot of peaceful land, dotted with knobby trees, cooled by a breezy Iberian climate' creates a carefully managed image.

THESE QUAKITY PIGS EVENTUALLY MAKE THEIR WAY TO A SMALL TOWN CALLED JABUGO, HUELVA; whose sole existence is devoted to ham. Turning grapes into wine, olives into oil, or pigs into ham, the process can be simple, complicated … or deliberately mysterious. From start to finish, the ham-making process is quite straightforward: simply slaughter and cure with little more than salt and air. For most customers that is where the story begins and ends. Not true, let us look at some detail.

There's the acorns which fall from oak and cork trees during early October to early March. They are high in fat, a large percentage of which is unsaturated oleic fatty acid. Acorns also contribute to the ham's nutty flavour and aroma. Over 18 to 24 months, the pigs will root around the dehesa (farm), grazing on grass, mushrooms, bugs, herbs, whatever they can find. Come October the acorn-dropping season begins, and the pigs go into overdrive.

Pigs are then slaughtered. Legs, loins, and shoulders go toward making ham, the remaining fresh meat sold to butchers and restaurants. The ham-bound legs are then skinned, salted, rinsed, dried, and sent to the curing cellar, where they'll remain for about a year and a half. Super premium varieties stay for 3 years.

The curing cellar is an underground city of ham; step downstairs and an aroma that's something between yeasted bread and aged cheese awaits. Thick brick walls, stable temperature, controlled humidity, and a population of ham-friendly microorganisms do their work to turn the legs into ham.

A quality check! With a short, stubby needle the 'ham sniffer' pokes down to the bone, quickly takes a smell, then covers the hole with a smear of fat. Just a second or two to detect the sign of a well-cured ham. The hams now move into a grateful consumer world, either whole or sliced.

Jamon Iberico shouldn't be sliced by machine – the soft fat would sheer and the lean, bony legs make horizontal slicing difficult – so clients need training in how to slice by hand. Like cutting salmon slices for smoking, or fish for sushi, carving Spanish ham is an artisan job of its own. The perfect slice is nearly transparent, small enough to eat in one bite and carved at an angle to obtain the greatest number of slices per leg.

WHILE JABUGO IS DEVOTED TO HAM, SO TO IS TREVELEZ HIGH IN THE ALPUJARRA'S. What makes Trevelez so interesting is just getting there. The route takes in Lanjaron (bottled water), Orgiva (home to the book Driving over Lemons), and a scenic, precipitous, narrow, twisting road, until a sign, depicting a leg of ham, signifies Trevelez. The town has a number of ham processing plants, a museum, accommodation and a restaurant that serves a gigantic mountaineer's lunch of black pudding, chorizo sausage, several slices of jamon, two fried eggs and potatoes. It is also one of the gateways on foot to the Mulhacen, the highest mountain in Spain.

LOCATIONS

Jabugo, Huelva.
Map reference 37 5504 N, 6 4342 W.
Nearest town - Huelva
Trevelez, Granada.
Map reference 37 0005 N, 3 1559 W.
Nearest town Lanjaron.

55. MADRID
chocolate and churros

ITS CHOCOLATE AND CHURROS, INDICATING HOT STICKY CHOCO-LATE HEATED to around 75°C, served in a porcelain cup accompanied by a plate of six to eight freshly made churros. It is usually accompanied with an envelope of sugar to sprinkle on the churros and a jug of cold water to quench a sudden thirst which appears afterwards. Consumption is simple, a churro is taken, sprinkled in sugar, and then dipped into the hot chocolate. The chocolate that remains after eating the churros is drunk.

A place where you can have chocolate with churros is in a churrera, usually a building with abundant blue marble decoration which is partly reminiscent of the 19th century, or typical of yesteryear. The smell in churrera's is a strange mixture between frying churros and boiling cocoa. It is an early morning breakfast, or a snack, or a night-time treat, with the usual social act of sitting around marble tables to converse with a neighbour.

Each churrera has its own ambience and a different way of making churros. In some places they are elongated, in others folded or in a ring. Some fry the dough with or without powdered sugar. It is a matter for the owner's taste, the diners too. Generally, churros are prepared when requested, thus making them crispy fresh. No owner reveals his secret formula relying on legions of fans who defend it as the best in town.

But many argue it is not the churros but the chocolate that makes this concoction delicious. During convivial conversation, accompanied by a portion of churros with its restorative cup of chocolate costing about 5€, little secretes pop out. Of course, it contains water, cocoa and some milk, quantities undisclosed but… utter sacrilege, the cocoa used is none other than the well-known Valor brand.

MADRID IS HOME TO SAN GINES, A SYMBOL OF THE CITY which serves one of the best chocolate and churros. With a century of history behind them, beginning in 1894, this signature place takes its name from the passage in which it is located. Difficult to find, it is not the only name by which this place has been known. 'The Hidden' is a better name. Nevertheless, San Gines reputation has made them a visitor attraction; a guide who does not embrace a visit or a mention, is rare indeed.

Despite the passage of time, San Gines has more or less remained the same. The marble of its bars and tables, walls covered with mirrors and green wooden frames, are all hallmarks of this emblematic corner of Madrid frequented by ordinary people, politicians and artists. Famous people have filled hanging face frames for posterity. Excepting Mark Zuckerberg, creator of Facebook, who visited the chocolate shop with his wife but opposed being photographed. However, many other actors and directors were simply happy to be photographed, such as film director Almodovar and even former President of the United States, Jimmy Carter.

The author, plus a family of three decided to visit San Gines one Sunday morning at 8.00. The taxi driver said, 'I'll drop you off here. It is down that lane, take another lane to the right. It is on a corner. You can't miss it.' No one was around. The streets were empty. Not even a cat or dog. Was this the correct place? The front door was pushed open to an avalanche of noise, smell, and heat, generated by a multitude of people inside. Holding up a hand to indicate four people was greeted by a shake of the head. A reservation was required. Come back at 11.00, or better still at night.

LOCATION
Madrid.
Map reference 40 2501 N, 3 4224 W. Capital of Spain.
San Gines – take a taxi.

56. SPANISH BAR
where to now?

'LA MONTANA' HAD NEW STAINLESS-STEEL TABLES OUTSIDE; occupied by English residents dressed in Hawaiian shirts and Spanish women all talking loudly at the same time. Powerful smells mingled together to form a distinctive aroma of Spanish bar life: beer, food, stale cigarettes and wafting across it all, the smell of coffee. The Spanish women finished eating and reached for their packets of Marlboro cigarettes; more smoke wafted through the air

'Hola,' said the owner
'Cafe con leche and a bocadillo – queso and jamon – por favor'.

The bar owner prepared the food. In one hand he wielded a long sharp knife, in the other a half-smoked cigarette. It was an impressive act. The food arrived; it was eaten hungrily. The women left, leaving behind them a smell of smoke, and scattered on the floor, cigarette ash, and the expected pile of screwed-up paper napkins.

Going inside it was a normal male dominated environment serving beer, wine, and tapas. Dark, with basic tables and chairs, walls painted some time ago in a murky yellow colour or was it a murky brown? A stuffed boar's head adorned the wall; the shelves contained a variety of silver cups for football behind which were pictures of the teams. There was also a large picture of grandfather looking starched and bemused, of grandmother starched and not amused, a proud man holding a horse, of pretty granddaughters and daughters in their national costumes taken during one of many fiestas. Dotted around were gaming machines, dart boards, posters displaying ice creams, boxes of crisps, wines, beer, and spirits. The top of the bar was littered with plates, cups and saucers, glasses, bottles, and the remains of food. Up high was a TV with no one watching bullfighting repeats. Was this typical Spanish culture or an unhygienic nightmare?

IT IS A COMMONPLACE BELIEF THAT SPAIN IS A LAND OF BARS, yet this is increasingly less so as the number of establishments are falling all the time. And the trend will continue. The industry blames not just a recent economic crisis, but also demographic shifts such as a rural exodus and an aging population. 'La Montana' is one of about 18,000 such like bars in Spain but for older bars it is becoming a fine line between traditional and run down. Many bars conform to their traditional image of a cosy place, where everyone talks to each other, to the owner, or waiter, as if they were best friends. Some things that do not change. But unless bars change from their past and attract a new crowd, their future is bleak.

If traditional rural bars are an old marketplace, then city centre coffee shops embracing a culture of western society, are the new marketplace. Spanish coffee culture exists; it has a few peculiarities, adjusted to their way of life, for coffee shops are seldom chains such as Starbucks or Costa. They are often small businesses, where you can speak and connect directly with the owner. Over time,  by frequenting one place people will learn preferences, owners call customers by their name and gently pull a person into the community of the shop.

People coming to work will have a coffee before coming in, take a quick break mid-morning for another and have one after lunch or mid-afternoon. Now some of these could be made at home, but this is Spain - it's the chat that counts.

LOCATION – anywhere Spain

57. VALENCIA
growing paella rice

ONLY 10 KILOMETRES FROM VALENCIA IS THE ALBUFERA NATURAL PARK, a Mediterranean ecosystem with forests, rice fields and a huge lake. This Park is home to the largest lake in Spain, one of its most important wetland areas. The waters are traditionally worked by fishermen and rice growers, supplying ingredients and inspiration for the region's most succulent dishes - paella.

Made up of cultivated fields, water channels, rural roads, traditional buildings and the Albufera lake, it has roots in Arab heritage. This area has been shaped by an irrigation system supplied from the Turia River, a system of ditches and channels designed in medieval times, in which water flows by gravity from nearby hills, to the river and hence to the low-lying Park.

Here, 120 million kilos of rice are grown each year under the umbrella of the Regulatory Council of the D.O. Arroz de Valencia Guarantee of Origin. There are three main rice varieties which are ideally suited to the conditions of La Albufera called Bahia, Senia and Bomba. While cooking they absorb liquid really well, perfectly complementing their fundamental attribute as a flavour carrier.

Traditional rice farming lasts a whole year involving painstaking farming work which is carried out in four stages: preparation of land, sowing, hoeing, and harvesting. The fields are prepared with fertilizer in February, then flooded in April, after which the rice seedlings are planted in straight lines. During the summer months the fields are hoed and then, in September, when the plants have grown, the rice is harvested.

The cultivation of rice was brought to Spain in the 8th century by the Arabs. The region of La Albufera became a primary producer of this Asian cereal. Valencia rice is a short-grain rice used mainly for paella. It contains a high quantity of starch and when cooked is moist and sticky. Sometimes called 'rice pearl' this actually is a reference to starch concentration, which gives an unmistakable white colour.

TRY LOCAL GASTRONOMY AT THE VILLAGE OF El PALMAR for classic rice dishes such as Paella, Arroz al Banda, or Alli Pebre (made with eels freshly caught from the lake). El Palmar, is close to the city of Valencia, a charming place with restaurants set by the water's edge. It definitely embraces the idea that Spaniards love to eat out and socialize. This town with a population of just 800 people is home to more than 30 restaurants. Competition is fierce. Quality is high.

Paella is a traditional dish of Spain. A colourful mixture of saffron-flavoured rice and various meats, paella's name comes from the paellera, a flat, round pan in which it is cooked. Traditionally, paella is cooked out of doors, over a wood fire. To make a paella, first saute meats, such as chicken, pork, rabbit, or seafood such as  clams, shrimps, mussels, crayfish, and squid. Use olive oil and season with onions, garlic, and herbs. Next, cook rice, tomatoes, and saffron, simmering over a low heat. Finally, mix in the meats or seafood and garnish with beans, pimientos, and other vegetables.

Questioning what makes a good paella is extremely contentious. There's one thing most paella enthusiasts in Spain seem to agree on. The sunny, fluffy, yellow rice dish served at Spanish restaurants all over the world, or the version topped with red peppers and loaded with everything from shrimp to chorizo to lobster, is not the real thing. Real Spanish paella, which is to say Valencia-style paella, is an altogether darker, richer, smokier creation: denser than pilaf, drier than risotto, and arguably more satisfying than either. What is the widely accepted original recipe for a dish that has remained constant through the ages? The original Valenciana paella dating back to the early 1800s, consists of saffron-scented rice cooked with rabbit, chicken, local snails, and three types of beans.

UNUSAL HOUSES CAN BE SEE IN EL PALMAR INCLUDING THE VALENCIAN BARRACA. They were once home to farmers and

fishermen, but now very few remain and of course they have become great icons of Valencian history. They are built from local materials such as mud, reeds, and wood but with little masonry walls.

And finally, ideal place to finish off a beautiful day exploring La Albufera and El Palmar is a small lookout at Dehesa del Saler. From here you can witness breath-taking sunsets sitting at a small dock, where people of all ages experience a magical evening.

LOCATIONS – all close to Valencia

Albufera National Park.
Map reference 39 1951 N, 0 2156 W.

El Palmar.
Map reference 39 1832 N, 0 1904 W.

Dehsa del Saler.
Map reference 39 2058 N, 0 1841 W.

WALKS

58. FUNTE DE
knocking on heaven's door

INCREASING NUMBERS OF PEOPLE ARE DISCOVERING THE DEEP GREEN LANDSCAPE, the solitude of the mountains and even the quiet sandy beaches of Northwest Spain. The Atlantic coast from the Portuguese border to the Pyrenees is dramatically scenic, wet and mild, creating lush green meadows and forests. In Asturias and Cantabria, the most obvious attraction is the group of mountains called the Picos de Europa which straddles the two communities. The Picos offer excellent hiking, but in winter when covered in snow, they are extremely dangerous.

The optimum time to visit the Picos is in summer. Winding roads and hiking trails are surprisingly quiet. Only the main town of Potes feels busy. The Picos seem to have stayed beneath hikers' radar. This may be down to the preconceived ideas that Europeans associate with Spain - heat, beaches, sea and Moorish architecture, not  craggy, Atlantic mountains, and snow. The Picos are still a busy farming area but times are changing fast. Abandoned stone villages, farmhouses and animal pens now sit beside perfectly refurbished holiday homes.

Teleferico Fuente De is a cable car in the heart of the Picos that whisks people up a nearby cliff face to a height of 1,823 metres where incredible panoramic views are enjoyed over the valley below. The cable car can carry 20 passengers at a time, climbing 753 metres in 3 minutes 40 seconds, thus avoiding the exhausting hassle of climbing. It is the longest cable car in Europe with a single section (unsupported wires) climbing almost vertically as it nears the end. Early morning on certain days inversion occurs, where the cable car bursts through clouds with the valley below obscured in white mist.

Fortunately, the Teleferico Fuente De is well-managed; buy a ticket, get a number, wait in a queue (a long queue) until the number is called, then go. Waiting is probably the only time to experience crowds, but waiting is yet another Kodak opportunity. So, lie down on green grass, chill out, look at multi coloured hikers with huge backpacks and observe the beauty of massive surrounding mountains.

There are many options on exit from the cable car. One is simply to walk around a bit then go back down. Another is to follow some of the high trails winding through gulley's to mountain hut accommodation. However, one of the regions classic downhill walks starts here. It has to be done. The views are spectacular, on this wonderful 9-kilometre hike, past craggy mountains with pockets of snow, eagles soaring overhead, descending into a lush green oak forest. The shattered limestone landscape is home to alpine flora and fauna, choughs, griffon vultures, snow finches and the occasional chamois

From the top of the cable car, descend past Refugio de Aliva, then Puertos de Aliva (mountain pasture grazed by cattle, horses and sheep in summer), then through meadows and forests of the Nevandi River valley, then down to the road at Espinama where refreshments can be obtained. All that remains is a return to Funte De. No problem thumb a lift, or cross the Rio Deva, pass through the village of Pido, then climb through superb limestone meadows and beech forests, before reaching Fuente De again.

The whole route is enjoyed by only a handful of other hikers all walking in the same clockwise direction, but beware, this can be deceptively dangerous country, so directions are necessary. It is also wise to check the timings of the cable car.

LOCATION

Funte De, Cantanbria.
Map reference 43 0839 N, 4 4801 W. Nearest town – Potes.

59. L'ORCA
old railway line

IN 1889, AN ENGLISH COMPANY 'ALCOY AND GANDIA RAILWAY AND HARBOUR COMPANY LTD' built a railway line to link the towns of Alcoy and Gandia. It was a prodigious feat of engineering necessitating the building of many tunnels, cuttings, and bridges. From then on the transport of merchandise from the hinterland to the coast was possible. Paper, textiles, oil, fruits, and vegetables were exported. Imported from England were coal and salt. The so-called 'English train,' running next to the fast flowing Serpis River, soon attracted paper mills and electric power generation. However from 1969 the line ceased to operate.

RECENTLY, A SCENIC PART OF THIS LINE HAS FORMED THE SERPIS GREENWAY, sometimes known as the 'Raco del Duc,' running from L'orca to Villalonga. Here is industrial heritage by the bucketful. Along the way are many railway artifacts, some of which are attached to walls and cuttings. Next to the river are abandoned ruins of old paper and flour mills. Uniquely old 'Light factories' with weirs can be visited. 'Light Factories' was a name given to small hydroelectric plants along the banks of a river.

Surrey, England in 1881, saw the construction of a modest and rudimentary mini-hydroelectric plant, equipped with a generator. It was a huge success. A few years later, at Raco del Duc, five mini-hydroelectric power stations were built based on this system. These plants, generated a voltage of between 11V and 20V, taking advantage of small dams where the river was redirected by canals to waterfalls. The force of the waterfall turned a turbine, which transmitted energy to a generator, transforming it into electricity. The use of energy generated by these power stations was fed to local industry along the river, in particular driving growth of a specialised paper industry (smoking paper and tissue paper widely used to wrap oranges).

Always accompanied by the sound of flowing water this old, abandoned train line is a rewarding journey explored easily on foot. From the level track there is a marked contrast between sheer cliffs surrounding the gorge and the gentleness of the river flowing through it. Picnicking, botanising, birdwatching, or looking at large fish swimming in pools, are the order of the day. And of course, observing a wealth of industrial heritage.

With 12 kilometres one way and another 12 kilometres back, absolutely no navigational skills are required. Start the walk from L'Orxa station, opposite an abandoned paper mill, following the old railway line just below a castle. History comes thick and fast. Here is the sequence:

Ruined house - Tunnel - Dam - Old hydroelectric station - Bridge - Hydroelectric station (now a water quality control station) - Old, ruined bridge - Short tunnel - Tunnel not much more than a wide arch – Bridge - Long tunnel - Last long tunnel.

High above the river the railway track passes through pine woods, until the end is reached - a dismantled bridge. Since there is no longer a way to cross the deep gorge below, it is necessary to return by the same route to L'orxa station.

THE STORY DOES NOT END HERE. One of eight locomotives constructed in Manchester in 1890, that once traversed the Alcoy to Gandia railway from its inception, sits proudly next to the main road through Alcoy, in a square called Plaça al Azraq. Named after one of the stations on the line, they were constructed by the Beyer, Peacock Company, specifically designed to suit the twisty route. The wheel arrangement was 2-6-2.

While there is nothing stopping visitors from climbing onto the footplate, be aware this is not officially sanctioned. The brass parts have been removed, so the big shiny, black locomotive, although impressive to view, is not preserved in working order.

LOCATIONS

L'orca, (can be spelt Lorcha or L'orxa), Alicante Province.
Map reference 38 5039 N, 0 11838 W. Nearest large town - Gandia,
Alcoy, Alicante Province.
Map reference 38 4156 N, 0 2352 W. Nearest large town - Gandia

60. SIERRA ESPUNA
disused railway tunnel

WHEN IT IS TIME TO GET AWAY FROM HEAT VISIT THE SIERRA ESPUNA. West from Murcia and east from Granada, siting at an average height of 800 metres, the authentic green lung of the region is a high place to enjoy peace and solitude.

Information in this region sometimes refers to a disused railway cutting and tunnel situated high up between Gerbas and El Berro (the Watercress) The only significance of Grebas is a hotel; nothing else. Conversely in a smart, clean, mountain village called El Berro, sits a newish camp site, the economics of which have apparently saved the village. The sixty-five-year-old female general store proprietor enthusiastically imparted some information - seven locals had died here in the first six months of this year, leaving only 134. At her youthful age she felt 'her maker' would exempt her from such a fate. It must be said, the tranquillity of El Berro endorses old age, such that a hospice or fertility clinic are as useless as bad paella.

Finding this disused railway cutting and tunnel is not be easy. Consult the web for information, **www.walksinspain.org/walks/sierra-espuna** is recommended, although other walking guides are available. The general idea is to hike from El Berro to Gerbas and back again. Or vice versa. Since the hotel is in Gerbas, the appropriate route is Grebas - El Berro – Grebas. Six kilometres there and six back in a sort of circular direction.

In summer, morning dawns at six o'clock. Complete stillness except for chirping birds. No movement other than scurrying lizards seeking basking rocks. A smell of freshness like new mown hay. Blue sky of course, no white cumulus, the mercury rising fast. The walk Grebas to El Berro is unremarkable, mainly up, up, and up 300 metres through pine trees, interspersed with scrubland, and then down a steep track into scorching hot El Berro.

It's surprising to find such a good restaurant in this remote mountain village. Like most property here the building is welded into the hillside. A place not to hurry, to eat and drink slowly, enjoying the surroundings together with regional food. At 9€ for 'menu del dia' with pan, wine, or water, it is regional cooking at its best.

Read closely the instructions for the return leg - El Berro to Grebas via a disused railway cutting and tunnel. 'Continue on a path straight ahead through fields and orchards. The path then becomes a track which ends at the start of a covered water culvert. Continue along the line of this culvert. Turn left down a path to intersect a deep cutting just before the valley floor. What appears to be a disused railway cutting and train tunnel come into view'.

Hikers will soon discover the instructions are correct. The covered water culvert was soon encountered; in fact, it was a continuous old stone water trough, containing a large plastic pipe filled with fast moving water, covered by curved stones which are difficult to walk upon. A very narrow path ran along the left of the culvert with a big vertical drop to the left and a two-meter drop into the culvert on the right. This was dangerous!

Soon it was there, a narrow, winding, abandoned railway line cut through steep rock, passing through a dark tunnel, then over a couple of avalanches blocking the way. It was eery, strangely cool, surprisingly twisty, walking along a railway track shared with high trees growing where trains should be. What on earth was it for? It must be  something to do with water, but what? Apparently it was a hydro project abandoned before it was completed. Things like this always seem to have been touched by the hand of Franco – but who knows.

The disused rail track ends at a gorge; nowhere to go, a missing bridge. But for the foot weary it was up a hill, down the other side and home to Grebas, thirsty, exhausted, satisfied.

In any major city, commuters wedge themselves into sweaty trains, bracing themselves for another day at the office, sitting in traffic jams, punching clocks, or switching on computers. Not so here, for time has not touched Sierra Espuna. It is relatively the same as when the ice age retreated, or when fighting took place for no good reason. This is an enchanted, calm place at ease with itself.

LOCATIONS – both close to Murcia
El Berro, Murcia.
Map reference 37 5321 N, 1 2940 W
Gerbas, Murcia. (only feature is Hotel Mariposa)
Map reference 37 5351 N, 1 2713 W.

61. FOUR CLASSIC WALKS
scary, grassy and scenic

EL CAMINIO DEL REY. A relatively short drive inland from the Costa del Sol with its glorious beaches and resort towns, an adrenaline adventure of a lifetime awaits, but not advisable for those with a fear of heights. 'El Caminito del Rey' is definitely a must do for the brave only.

Pinned along the sheer walls of a gorge at El Chorro, near Alora in Malaga province, the 'King's little path' is a daring walk, high above the river which flows below. This narrow wooden footpath is a maximum of one metre wide and runs for 7.7km, rising in some parts to over 100 metres in height.

Ironically, it wasn't always an adventure walkway. It was originally built to give workers at the hydroelectric power plants at Chorro Falls and Gaitanejo Falls a means of access. Construction on the walkway started in 1901 and was completed in 1905. It was in 1921 when King Alfonso XIII completed the walkway for an inauguration ceremony when it received its current name.

The footpath fell into disrepair some years ago after five hikers died in 1999 and 2000. It was closed, many thought forever but it was eventually decided to make extensive repairs. The walkway reopened in March 2015, much to the delight of daredevils and adrenaline junkies alike. Tickets to experience the walk of a lifetime are free, but please note a need to reserve in advance. This is a popular experience, with numbers regulated at any one time.

THE RUTA DEL CARES was opened between 1945 and 1950 with a single objective - the operators of the Camarmena hydroelectric power plant required access to water channels that reach the Cain dam. About

45 workers worked on this complicated project, which together with a canal, is carved out of rock some 50 metres above the Cares river. Workers had to open about 75 tunnels, most of them in the second section of the route just before reaching Cain. In addition, bridges were built to cross the ravine from one side to the other.

This most spectacular route separates Asturias and Leon through the heart of the Picos de Europa National Park. The path runs between the towns of Poncebos (Asturias) and Cain (Leon), or vice versa as it can be done in reverse. The 12 kilometres one-way track is practically flat, running along a path of one to three metres wide with vertical rock on one side and a precipice on the other. Be careful if you have vertigo!. Starting in Poncebos the initial slope is a bit hard. Starting in Cain, it will all be downhill.

There is one big important difference between El Camino del Rey and the Ruta del Cares. In the former there is a handrail to prevent people falling into the gorge. In the later there is no handrail.

COVODONGA. If verdant green hills, snow-capped peaks and green grass are your thing, you don't need to go to the Alps. The Picos de Europa

fits the bill perfectly and is home to dozens of fabulous hiking routes, among them the stunning Covadonga Lakes trail.

This is a beautiful circular route around the religious shrine at Covadonga. Starting at the Covadonga Sanctuary, it is 12 kilometres to the first of the lakes, Lake Enol. However, this can be shortened in summer by bus. Although it can be busy crowds soon melt away. The circular route goes past some of the region's most peaceful lakes, with lookout points along the way. The path is quite flat, easy with lots of short green grass alongside.

LOS CAHORROS, MONACHIL, GRANADA. A tranquil, lesser-known alternative to Caminito del Rey lies further to the north, just outside the spectacular city of Granada. The Los Cahorros Gorge in the Monachil River Valley is one of the Sierra Nevada's most picturesque hiking routes and, despite the dramatic hanging bridges and overhanging rocks, the walk itself is quite safe and easy. The hike will take about four hours through nine kilometres of breath-taking scenery in one of Spain's most iconic mountain range

LOCATIONS

El Camino del Rey, Malaga.
Map reference 36 5604 N, 4 44804 W.
Nearest town - Malaga.

Ruta del Cares, Picos.
Map reference 43 1520 N, 4 5008 W.
Nearest town - Gangas.

Covodonga, Picos.
Map reference 43 1619 N, 4 5929 W.
Nearest town - Gangas.

Monachill, Granada.
Map reference 37 0756 N, 3 3225 W.
Nearest city Granada.

PAY A VISIT

62. ANDORRA
shop till you drop

THE PRINCIPALITY OF ANDORRA IS A SMALL INDEPENDENT COUNTRY with 75,000 inhabitants and 8 million annual tourists who ski, enjoy mountain activities and go shopping. Some say Andorra is simply another fast road joining France to Spain through high mountain country. It certainly contains lots of snow, concrete and many car parking spaces. To many, its weather makes it a place of greyness. No sun worshipers here, just big Wellie shops to plough through the slush. Snow-capped mountains and green summer pastures do however add a sense of beauty.

Andorra is for shopping, eating and nature trails, or in winter for shopping, eating, and skiing. Note the emphases on shopping. Even if people dream about going on vacation for unparalleled skiing, or thrilling mountain bike runs, or steep hiking trails, shopping is often how they spend some time. In this regard Andorra does not disappoint.

The best way to capture the scale of Andorra shopping is to note that there are roughly 2,000 stores packed into a country which you can drive through in about half an hour. Those numbers become even more striking when you realise most of Andorra's shopping centres are concentrated in the capital, Andorra la Vella. Women and men's fashion, jewellery, watches, accessories, sporting goods, food and drink, are what people go for. And of course, cheap cigarettes and liquor which are so popular that it's not uncommon for major supermarkets to devote 25% of their space stocking these items.

There are two golf courses in Andorra; Europe's highest, accessed by a gondola chair lift, obviously closed during winter by snow. Set in spectacular, flattish ground at high altitude the ball goes far, convincing a player of dramatic game improvement.

Something else hits you in Andorra apart from the cold and mist. There is nothing to put your hand up to say, 'Andorra, this is a great country.' Things are pristine, organised, everything in its place, no litter of graffiti but something else is lacking. No laughter, no McDonald's wrappers in the streets, no alcohol fuelled guys sitting in doorways, and no cafe culture. It is an emptiness. Being squeezed between cultural France and gregarious Spain, rather than absorbing two cultures, it has eliminated both.

The author on leaving Andorra heading back to Spain, met a female border guard who was intent on him staying. He stopped at a red light on the border and waited for about five minutes. Nothing happened so he drove on. Whistle! Wait, again nothing happened. Suddenly confrontation!

'Where do you think you are going?'

At least I think that is what she said. Was it French, Spanish or something else?

'I'm waiting for you,' I said.

'Open boot.' She stood there, white pallor, 100 kilos, gun, truncheon, phone, gold braid.

'Cigarettes?'

'Don't smoke.'

She rummages through the boot - nothing.

'Next time you stop at red light.'

'What next time?'

LOCATION

Andorra.

Map reference 42 3028 N, 1 1316 E.

Nearest large town – Perpignan, France.

63. BARCELONA
up top and below

AT EACH END OF LAS RAMBLAS ARE BARCELONAS FAMOUS LANDMARKS. At the top is the grand Placa de Catulunya, a square that occupies some 50 000 square metres and is widely considered to be the city's central point. At the lower end, towards the waterfront is the Columbus monument. This 60-metre-tall, stone column is a local meeting point with Columbus standing proudly on top pointing out to sea. In the middle is La Boqueria market, also known as Mercat Sant Josep, a world-renowned indoor market situated right next to a metro stop.

La Ramblas is a living, breathing, 24-hour place where anything is possible. Let's face it, if you're looking for things to do in Barcelona, you will with-out-doubt find yourself on Las Ramblas at some point.

People working on this street are diverse, charismatic and a little strange. Street artists, street art and street performers line Las Ramblas and create an utterly unique vibe. There are street performers in many other European cities, but Barcelona is the authority on this industry. For those who are not familiar with street performers, look at a man painted entirely in white, wearing his favourite white hat and a pair of white Y- fronts sitting on a toilet, reading the local paper in the middle of the street!

Some of these Barcelona street artists have been doing this type of job for years. Top of the range are performers who seem to defy balance by sitting on a single stick. It is difficult to imagine Las Ramblas without these crazy, clever, sometimes beautiful street performers and it certainly doesn't look as though they are going anywhere soon.

Las Ramblas florists offer a more romantic service, selling beautiful fresh cuttings all day long. Known as the Rambla de le Flora they add colour and vibrancy to Las Rambla and a sweet floral scent too. Towards the bottom artists showcase their paintings. With fierce competition some really high-quality paintings are available for seriously low prices. These paintings are ideal souvenirs and definitely more original than generic T-shirts snapped up everywhere.

Las Ramblas by night is a different story. Take care! You will find some shady characters stroll past without making eye contact and mutter, Marijuana, Cocaine, Hashish. Ignore them! Even making eye contact will encourage pestering. These people move in the same circles as pickpockets. Most of these 'unsavoury characters' hang out around the bottom end of Las Ramblas.

A PLETHORA OF REASONS IS WHY BARCELONA IS A MOST POPULAR DESTINATION. One of the biggest reasons being the extraordinary works of the world-famous Catalan architect Antoni Gaudi. The Sagrada Familia is one of the most famous landmarks in Europe. Gaudi took over construction in 1883 until he died in 1926. The basilica is still currently under construction and financed by the cost of tour tickets with the plan to finish in 2026. This massive gothic style basilica has vastly different styles on each facade so when visiting it is important to take a thorough walk around each side.

The interior of the Sagrada Familia is equally as impressive as the exterior with a vast amount of colourful glass, which bathes the entire basilica in a variety of colours with a hint of sunlight. Almost every part of the interior, as well as the exterior, symbolizes something of religious significance. When visiting take a tour to fully understand the deep and rich symbolism throughout this incredible structure.

Other Barcelona creations by Gaudi well worth visiting too include: Casa Batllo, Casa Mila La Pedrera, Park Guell, Palau Guell and Casa Calvet.

CHRISTOPHER COLUMBUS, THE DISCOVER OF AMERICA, OVERLOOKS LAS RAMBLAS. Although America was first discovered by Icelanders 500 years earlier, Columbus is still considered in history to be the discoverer of the continent. A permanent colonization of the American continent began – so did suppression, destruction of its indigenous people and robbery of their treasures.

Born in Genoa in 1451 his original mission was to find a sea route from Europe to East Asia. He himself thought he had landed in India. But on October 12, 1492, Columbus landed on a Bahamian island. He undertook a total of four trips to America, returning from the last on the 7th of November 1504. He died on May 20th, 1506 and is reputed to be buried in Sevilla.

The Columbus Monument was inaugurated on the occasion of the World Fair on 1 June 1888. After a lengthy overhaul, the Monument was re-opened to the public in June 2013. The 60-meter-high emblematic monument is situated at the bottom of Las Ramblas. There is a small elevator inside the tower going to the top with a 360 degree walk round.

AT MONSERATT THERE ARE CURRENTLY SOME 80 SAINT BENEDICT MONKS.

The interior of the monastery, in part of the museum, sits an exceptional library with a collection of more than 250,000 volumes.

The view from the Monastery is spectacular. It is the highlight of a visit. Marked rocky trails can take a visitor even higher. Equally amazing

is how this immense building has been carved into rock.

A feature always associated with the monastery of Montserrat is the Escolania, one of the oldest boys' choirs in Europe, with documents from the 14th century speaking of its existence. It consists of a choir of boys between 10 and 14 years of age who sing at various religious services.

Montserrat is an extremely popular visitor destination, many of them on a day trip from Barcelona. When purchasing tickets to Montserrat at Barcelona Espana Station it is necessary to purchase the correct type of ticket.

There are two versions. One ticket for a route by Cable Car. The other ticket is to go up to the Monastery by the Cremallera Funicular.

A monk's life is devoted to prayer and work. They can be distinguished from other orders of Monks by their philosophy that there is an importance to everything. The Monks listen to the voice of God through both the Holy Scriptures, developments in the Church and what happens in the world. The Monks live in a building that sits just to the left of the Montserrat Basilica. It can be accessed from the Atrium of the Basilica, but it is not open to the public. It is possible to write to a monk!

AS A CULTURE CONTRAST, BARCELONA'S HISTORIC 19TH CENTURY UNDERGROUND SEWERS, whose foundations were laid in medieval times, are now open to the public. Originally the Aqueduct-based sewer system was introduced to Barcelona, an ancient Roman colony, because when it rained the whole city would flood. Much later, in 1364 medieval architects expanded the sewers and ran water beneath Las Ramblas.

It wasn't until 1886 that Pere García Faria designed the first modern sewers in the city. Today some of these tunnels are still in use. Most are inaccessible to the public, but thanks to a dedicated group of Barcelonian tour guides, some sewers are open for adventuring. The best remnants are located below Passeig San Joan. Beneath these streets, a whole world opens up. The quiet flow of water in the dank sewers is illuminated by dim fluorescent lights while the city's hustle and bustle continues above.

Visits are organised by La Fabrica del Sol. Small groups (no more than fourteen) are guided by locals who explain the evolution of the aquatic tunnels, their technical processes, engineering and other curiosities.

LOCATION
Barcelona.
Map reference 41 2309 N, 2 1023 E.

64. BULNES
village without a road

UNTIL RECENTLY, BULNES WAS ONLY REACHED BY AN UPHILL MEANDERING PATH, carved between steep mountains of extraordinary beauty. People, mules, food and supplies and mail regularly travelled this route. A route that hardly had a function in winter when it was hidden by snow and a helicopter was required for an occasional urgency, or mountain rescue.

But now, the last town without road access in Asturias, can be reached by an underground sloping tunnel in just seven minutes. From 2001, its residents, visitors and mountaineers, enjoy a funicular (a cable train), which runs through a rectilinear tunnel of 2,227 metres climbing the limestone of the Picos de Europa, from Poncebos to Bulnes.

What is a funicular? It's a special type of railway track used to climb steep slopes, quite common throughout Europe. It runs on two sets of rails, one cabin going up while the other comes down. The cabins are joined by a steel cable.

Bulnes is worth a visit for many reasons, whether by funicular or on foot. In this village there is an unusual atmosphere, a rustic reality in which few people can be seen. It holds a good number of Asturian houses set close together in a village that now sees tourist services as its main source of income. Along these narrow alleyways lie a handful of charming small restaurants, shops, and lodgings, serving cabrales blue-cheese and fabada. But despite low-level tourism having reached Bulnes, it's still a place to find yourself utterly entranced by one of Europe's most remote villages.

It should not be overlooked that this village, where no more than 40 people live, was founded by roaming shepherds who one day decided to live here permanently. They still use pack donkeys to transport artisan cheeses down to market and carry up unwieldy butane gas bottles in the opposite direction.

The village is perched 649 metres high, surrounded by huge summits. Bulnes serves as a jumping of point to the famous Pico Urriellu (Naranjo de Bulnes), a major classic challenge for mountaineers from all over the world. The starting point for the funicular, or walk, is at Hotel Mirador de Cabrales in Puente Poncebos which as the Americans say is a trailhead from Arenas de Cabrales. It is also the starting point for the famously scary Cares Gorge walk. With so many options It can get crowded in summer.

LOCATION

Bulnes, Picos.
Map reference 43 1407 N, 43910 W.
Nearest town - Gangas.

65. CASTELL DE CASTELLS
typical village at a crossroads?

SERELLA CASTLE (ALSO KNOWN AS EL CASTELLET) IS AN AMAZING RUIN located on the rocky outcrop crest of Sierra Serella (1050 m). To the north it looks down on the village of Castell de Castells; to the south a touristic village of Guadalest with its associated reservoir. The ruins of Serrella Castle are hard to spot at first, but once you locate the obvious impressive rock across the valley from Castells you have a good chance of seeing what remains of its walls.

The first record of the castle was 1244. The Castle and its population were of Muslim origin. It is one of a string of major castles, including its associated lands and various farmsteads, mentioned in the Pact of la Jovada ceded to the Moorish head man, al-Azraq. It was retaken by King Jaime 1 in 1254 and abandoned soon after the Christian re-conquest It sits, gazing down like an ancient sentinel, on to the village known today as Castell de Castells.

The castle is a ruin, but those with a head for heights can see remains of its walls and a water cistern which still holds rain. The ruined tower still stands at height of about 4m. The lower walled refuge is a large space bordered by the remains of a low wall. Hikers can reach it by a stiff climb from Castells or Guadalest.

Wild orchids, rosemary, fennel, thyme and sage grow in abundance in this mountain microclimate. On the lower slopes, olive and almond trees bathe in sun drenched terraces; many of them still tended today by old fashioned methods handed down through generations. Small, green, ancient tractors till the barren soil – part of Franco's heritage –

the so-called economic miracle of self-sufficiency.

VISITORS HEADING INLAND FROM THE COAST ARE DISMAYED TO FIND HOW LITTLE ENGLISH is understood except by a small number of resident foreigners. Why should the other four hundred Spanish inhabitants even consider another language? Its knowledge is not a prerequisite to life in a land of thin air, crisp winter mornings or a hot searing summer sun.

The main church sits of course in the village square, which also has its inevitable bars. There are other places to spend a few euros; more bars, a butcher, a hairdresser, a chemist, a baker, two casa rurals, a good hotel, an excellent restaurant and a weekly market. They are required for everyday living; no disco bars or wild parties take place.

Castells is not overrun, that's impossible in its narrow streets virtually impenetrable to modern vehicles. Roads were built to the width of a donkey and cart (or two donkeys and two carts). Underneath 200-year-old houses provision was made for survival – they contained farm implements, cattle or poultry. The narrowness of its streets blocks direct sunlight waiting for shade at sunset. This is the time when a veil of heat lifts from the village, the parched hills of the surrounding sierra turn from green to brown and distant mountains change to dark blue.

At dusk, the old village falls strangely silent, apart from the church clock ringing. In warm weather, occupants sit outside their homes in the cobbled, narrow back streets and talk, for this is a friendly place where politeness, courtliness and happiness are in order. Then doors studded with brass buttons silently close. The reflected light of the occasional television screen flickers from a darkened interior.

Castells' Spanish residents are sons and daughters of the land, seeking a living from olive and almond trees while their brothers and sisters down the valley tend to their orange and lemon groves. Further down, working as a waiter in tourist dominated costal resorts, creates wealth and prevents unemployment. But life goes on much as before. Family ties remain. As the old die, they are solemnly laid to rest in niches, in a small cemetery surrounded by wildflowers, next to a crumbling, neglected building nearby.

CASTELLS, LIKE MANY OTHER VILLAGES IN SPAIN, IS AT A CROSSROADS. It is a template for a rural Spanish village. It is an hour by car from Alicante and Valencia but viewed from any perspective it is light years away. Will it move forward based on visitors attracted to hiking in the surrounding mountains?

Abundant facilities for swimming, petanque, boules and children's playgrounds, lie largely untouched. Locals like their bars, a pint of cerveca, a bocadillo, a noisy fiesta, but not a lot more. In the meantime, grocery shops close and bars change hands. Houses remain empty, undisturbed except for their crumbling interiors smelling of decay. Banks retreat leaving ATM's in their wake. Fields of almond and olives slowly return to nature. Inhabitants look to spend their money in big supermarkets or shopping malls a few kilometres down the valley. Old people die. The church bell tolls! The priest comes with remarkable alacrity. Another niche in the cemetery opens… and closes.

LOCATION

Castell de Castells, Alicante.

Map reference 38 4332 N, 0 1140 W. Nearest town Denia.

66. CORDOBA
a rich heritage, bullfighting posters and more

PEOPLE LIVING IN THE OLD QUARTER OF CORDOBA ARE LUCY ENOUGH TO WALK PAST one of Andalusia's most iconic buildings. The city's Mosque-Cathedral is the greatest dual-identity monument in Spain - a powerful symbol of two cultures that shaped Andalusia. After the Moors captured Cordoba in 711, what had previously been a Visigoth Christian church, was split in two and used by both Christians and Muslims as a place of worship. But in 784, on the orders of the Emir Abd al-Rahman, the church was destroyed, and work began on a great mosque. Construction lasted for over two centuries and the building was eventually completed in 987, by which point Cordoba was the most important city in the Islamic Kingdom.

When the city was reclaimed by the Christians in 1236, the mosque was converted into a church, and in the 16th century Charles V added a Renaissance nave on top of the Moorish structure. The mosque's most famous feature is its vast main hall, supported by over 850 double-arched columns. Sunlight and shadows create unusual effects as people wander among them, contemplating the complex history of this great building.

Even when compared to the oldest neighbourhoods of other major Andalusian cities, Cordoba is conspicuously charming, with its side-by-side white houses decorated with pots of aromatic jasmine and geraniums. Particularly attractive is the Calleja de las Flores, a narrow, winding lane lined with some of the prettiest and most colourful houses you'll find in Andalusia. Whilst wandering, look for this barrio's hidden treasures – namely, the private patios and courtyards that are opened to the public every May for the city's enchanting Feria de los Patios.

The Castle of the Catholic Kings is the kind of place Cordoba's locals probably take for granted, yet it is one of the city's key architectural landmarks. As its name suggests, the construction of this royal palace was ordered by the Catholic King Alfonso XI of Castile in 1328 but – as is so often the case in Andalusia – it was built amongst the ruins of a vast Moorish fort. In the late 10th century when the Islamic Kingdom was at the height of its power. Cordoba was one of the world's great intellectual cities.

It was not until the 1950s, when Cordoba's town hall was being expanded, that the remains of what was probably the city's most important Roman temple were discovered. Built during the reign of Emperor Claudius in the middle of the 1st century AD, and renovated in the 2nd century AD, the temple boasted a plethora of giant columns, 10 of which remain today, reaching up into the sky amid modern apartment blocks and offices.

Cordoba's famous Roman Bridge, or Puente Romano, dates from the 1st century BC and was extensively rebuilt in the 10th century. Sitting low over the opaque waters of the Guadalquivir, which flows all the way through Andalusia and out into the Atlantic, it is supported by 17 stone arches, of which just two once belonged to the original structure. The middle of the bridge, next to a 17th-century statue of Saint Raphael, is the perfect spot from which to survey Cordoba and the green, hilly countryside around.

IT IS BEST NOT TO THINK ABOUT THE MORALITY OF BULL FIGHTING. A lithe slip of a man squeezed into a tight suit, his only defence a red cape, and a sword facing six hundred kilos of testosterone concentrated into two frighteningly large, wide horns, with points as sharp as sabres. Everyone is aware in a bullfight several bulls are going to be injured in various ways. They will be lanced, they will have sharp barbs stuck in them, and in the end they will be killed, more or less efficiently, with a sword. There will be blood and there will be death. And if someone may be upset, or if they think it is barbaric and cruel, then it is really not worth going.

Cordoba is the home of bull fighting. It is also the home of a unique souvenir. A personalised bull fighting poster with the name of a want-a-be bullfighter printed at the bottom. To keep up with equality, this city has personalised flamenco posters for women too.

ENJOY SALMOREJO. EVERYONE HAS HEARD OF GAZPACHO, BUT LESS WELL KNOWN is a delicious variation on the famous summer dish that hails from Cordoba. Salmorejo, like its more ubiquitous cousin, is made from fresh tomato juice, olive oil and garlic – but it is thickened with breadcrumbs and usually topped with chunky wedges of cured jamon, croutons and slices of hard-boiled egg. Any tapas bar in Cordoba worth its salt will offer a homemade version of this local classic – often featuring the cook's individual twist – it makes for a refreshing, light lunch.

THE WIDE GUADALQUIVIR RIVERBED HOLDS SMALL ISLANDS WHICH TODAY ARE INHABITED BY BIRDS. Long ago there were flour mills, of which some remains can be seen to this day. One near the north riverbank is called Molino de la Albolafia. The waterwheel has appeared on Cordoba seals and other city emblems since the 13th century. A huge chain pump was built in order to take water up to the Alcazar Palace Gardens, but Isabella, the Catholic queen, had it taken down to avoid its annoying squeaking noise. What is seen today is a reconstruction.

Although its initial function was to provide irrigation water, it later became a flour mill. The external appearance of the mill remained unchanged between the 16th and 19th centuries. The wheel had several owners but was ultimately seized by the Government in 1914, becoming the property of the State.

In 1965, it was ceded to the Cordoba City Council who ordered a major reform of the complex. The large wheel was returned to its original state. The last intervention was carried out in 1992, when after suffering a fire, the waterwheel was rebuilt. The base of the mill was also evacuated to expose the original water channels.

LOCATION

Cordoba, Andalusia.

Map reference 37 5320 N, 4 4645 W. Regional capital

67. LE PERTHUS AND LA JONQUERA
supermarket sex

SOMEWHERE ALONG THE WAY THE GOVERNMENTS OF FRANCE AND SPAIN BECAME A bit confused. The border for Catalans was not clearly defined. Let's muddle through they must have said – that's how we do things here. But on this divided border some towns are half French and the other half Spanish.

Take for example Le Perthus on the N9, a strange no man's land dedicated to consumerism. Le Perthus, is a French border village in the Pyrenees so prosperous that the inhabitants pay almost no municipal taxes. And how do they earn their money? As a parking space! Every year, this village earns no less than 780,000 euros from day trippers who park their car in France and then go shopping in the much cheaper Spain just across the border.

Today stroll down the 'route principale' from the French side and you are still in France until you arrive at the stone marker, just past the town hall. At this point, it all depends which side of the road you are on! In fact, based upon a rather bizarre border agreement which dates to the signing of the Treaty of the Pyrenees, (1659) Le Perthus becomes Spanish on the left-hand side and French on the right. Difficult to know when to stop saying 'Bonjour' and start saying 'Holà'!

Most of the large shops on the left are Spanish with booze and tobacco ringing up at Spanish prices, which explains the permanent presence of sweaty, garlic smelling, jostling bodies pushing shopping trolleys full of Pastis and Saint Miguel along narrow, packed pavements, towards cars mainly parked in France. Dodgy dealers offer camcorders, watches, or sunglasses. The presence of street sellers surreptitiously touting their wares, only adds spice to a slightly seedy fairground feel.

Thrusting and trusting, bullying, and jostling
Pulling and pushing, shouting, and shushing
Rushing and puffing, dragging, and carrying
Smiling and crying, honeyed lips lying

Cheap beer and pastis and Cuban cigars
Lizards in alcohol and ladies in bars
Whisky and vodka and gin all flow
Street vendors hassling - so hard to say no

Little girls' eyes fixed on bright Spanish frocks
Flamboyant flamenco displayed in a box
Sombreros, paellas, and cheap leather tat
Dull-eyed cashiers calculating the VAT

OF COURSE, THERE IS A LOT MORE TO LE PERTHUS THAN CHEAP BOOZE, paella pans and sombreros! Go back and turn north, as you leave Le Perthus for France, follow signs to Fort de Bellegarde when the noise of cash registers dims, and the motorway lorries high above take on dinky toy proportions. Le Perthus was an important passage through the Pyrenees in Roman times. The route connected Rome with Cadiz and was part of 100,000 kilometres of roads built by the Romans throughout their mighty empire. Nearby, the tracks of the Roman wagon wheels are still visible; it is easy to close your eyes and imagine Hannibal crossing here in 281 BC. The true strategic importance of this fort enabled a series of uninterrupted wars between Spain and France for more than a hundred years. It is the oldest pass in the Eastern Pyrenees with an exceptional panorama over both countries.

A FEW KILOMETRES DOWN SOUTH, ON THE N9, LA JONQUERA SLIPS INTO VIEW: much the same as Le Perthus with a few extras. 'It's a supermarket for sex.' So says the mayor of La Jonquera. 'It is a sign of the times: we close down factories and open up brothels.'

A five-minute drive through La Jonquera is all it takes to understand the mayor's frustration over prostitution. There are semi-naked women everywhere under the bridges, on traffic circles, in parking lots, all trying to attract the attention of drivers. They can make up to 300 euros a day or nothing at all. They are there every day, rain, sun, or shine.

Once, this border town of 3,000 residents was something of a shopping destination for the French. Now this quiet little village with ochre coloured houses, has become a vast commercial zone. At a recent count there were 16 supermarkets, 400 stores, 46 restaurants and 16 service stations. Quite simply it is a frontier boom town built on low duty Spanish goods, where brothels are legal.

La Jonquera has become famous for its prostitution. Competition is fierce: there are the roadside prostitutes, with sun burnt skin. Their behinds are bare, the few items of clothing on their bodies garish and cheap. There is HGV sex, prostitutes operating uncontrolled in La Jonquera's huge HGV parks zigzagging their way between trucks. And there are those who work inside a giant brothel called Le Paradise, Europe's largest-ever brothel, with 80 rooms and up to 200 prostitutes.

If people can buy cheap alcohol, cigarettes, fuel and tyres, why not sex also? Not for nothing has Le Paradise been called a 'contemporary factory brothel.' At weekends, the clients of Le Paradise are overwhelmingly French from the neighbouring Languedoc-Roussillon.

The town opposed the brothel, whose owner was facing charges in two separate legal investigations when he requested a license. Local authorities turned down his request, but the Catalonia Superior Court of Justice forced them to award it. 'How can you give someone, who is facing legal charges, a license to open a brothel' people ask? Where does the poor mayor of La Jonquera stand in all this? Whilst acknowledging that sex supermarkets bring sales revenue and employment to the town (perfumeries, beauty technicians, hairdressing salons, pharmacies, doctors, taxis et al) he does not rejoice in this type of income.

The owner of Le Paradise makes his money by renting his rooms to young women at 70€ per room per day, the use of a gym and food included. He takes no percentage from their income, the women charge what they like, it's down to client negotiation in the two 'salles de spectacles' that together can accommodate 500 people.

LOCATIONS – these locations are almost joined together close to Perpignan, France.

Le Perthus, Girona.
Map reference 42 2747 N, 2 5152 E.
La Jonquera, Girona.
Map reference 42 2505 N, 2 5227 E.

68. GRANADA
the art of taracea

CONNOISSEURS OF THE ART OF MARQUETRY IN WHICH TINY PIECES OF COLOURED HARDWOODS are arranged into geometric patterns glued into wooden frames, may be interested in a demonstration at Laguna Taracea, Real de la Alhambra 30, just down from the Alhambra. On display in this shop are elaborately patterned, incredibly beautiful, trays, boxes, chess sets, picture frames, and more. Also available are large, heirloom-quality chests of drawers, each emulating a different 17th-century Iberian design selling for several thousand euros.

The art of wooden inlay or marquetry was brought to Granada from Northern Africa. Originally the designs would have inlaid shapes made from exotic woods, mother of pearl, tortoiseshell, ivory or bone. Precious stones nestle amongst exotic wood too. The head artisans in Granada are elderly eighty-year-old men; it´s the only job they have known. The technique of carving bone is particularly tough on their hands..

Marquetry, known in Spanish as Taracea comes from the Arab word ´Tarci´ which means to incrust. Since the 14th century Taracea has been produced in the city of Granada. That´s over 600 years ago. It´s the only place in Spain where it is still made, sadly seeming to be a dying art form.

It is a fiddly business. To begin with they make lots of star shapes. This consists of joining together many long rods of different woods. When the rods are set together they cut slices which make a star shape. They also make an edging which looks like tape. These strips are made from very thin strips of wood, made in a similar way to

the star rods, but cut horizontally along the length. Once they have the edging and the stars they can begin to design the work. Choose a wooden unfurnished box, or piece of furniture, draw the design, add all the pieces, press in a vice to set them into place, smooth the surface and then varnish.

It is possible to buy taracea souvenirs from as little as 15 euros or splash out with a grand writing bureau including secret drawers and scenes from the Alhambra palace. Favourites are little taracea chests or boxes with shiny white mother of pearl on top.

SHOPPING IN GRANADA DOES NOT STOP WITH TARACEA. NEED A GUITAR, SOME CASTANETS? Alcaiceria, once the Moorish silk market, is next to the cathedral in the lower city. The narrow streets of this rebuilt village of shops are filled with vendors selling the arts and crafts of Granada. The Alcaiceria offers one of the most splendid assortments of tiles, castanets and wire figures of Don Quixote chasing windmills. Lots of Spanish jewellery can be found here too.

Granada and the art of flamenco guitar making have always been intertwined. Even if you don't want a guitar from Andalusia, you might want to check out the neighbourhood where they're manufactured. Calle Cuesta de Gomerez, a narrow and steeply sloping street that runs downhill from the Alhambra is the centrepiece of the city's guitar-making trade. Today there are at least five guitar-making studios, generally small shops with no more than two, and usually only one, artisan per cubbyhole. Prices for the most basic instruments might, in a pinch, begin at 400€ with some of the most resonant guitars easily exceeding 3,500€.

LOCATION

Granada.
Map reference 37 0950 N, 3 2944 W. Regional Capital

69. MADRID
a fast day out

HOW TIME FLIES WHEN YOU'RE HAVING FUN, AND THIS TRAIN REALLY FLIES. But there's nothing frenetic about streaking down the middle of Spain at speeds of 300 km per hour. It's actually a relaxing journey, with time to read, nap, drink, eat and gather your thoughts about where to go. How often do we get a chance to really play it cool, riding a high-speed train? An illuminated digital sign over the carriage door displayed 300 km per hour. A little cheer went up! The countryside went whizzing past. White new wind farms came and went. La Mancha was a blur. This was the AVE train from Valencia to Madrid; how to travel a long distance in Spain without a car.

With 3,240km of track, Spanish high-speed AVE trains operate on the longest network in Europe This modern train system connects many cities from Madrid to Barcelona, Cordoba, Seville, Málaga, Alicante and Valencia.

The AVE stops at Atocha station. Carriage doors open, run up steps, all hustle and bustle. Madrid is full of buzz and culture. Artistically the city holds its own against any in Europe, with the best museums on the continent. There are also countless little things to make Madrid memorable, whether that's a cafe con leche in a stately square, drinks in a rooftop bar, or wandering through Retiro Park.

Let's list the best touristy things to do in Madrid:

The Prado, Retiro Park, Royal Palace, Santiago Bernabeu Stadium, National Archaeological Museum, Puerta del Sol, Gran Vía, Plaza Mayor, Mercado San Miguel, El Rastro, Thyssen-Bornemisza Museum of Art and the Reina Sofia Museum.

Which one? It's too hot to be wandering aimlessly around.

'LA PLAZA MAYOR POR FAVOUR' To understand a city like Madrid it is necessary to discover where it all began. Its epicentre. Its beating heart. Here the beauty of Madrid lies in an eclectic mix of architectural century-sweeping designs in La Plaza Mayor. This well-loved meeting place still buzzes with the same energy it did when it was constructed in 1617.

The fight for tourist pounds, euros or dollars is noticed immediately upon entering the Plaza. Waiters verbally attack potential customers visiting the emblematic square, without shyness, menu in hand, to get the next sale. One waiter yells at another:

'Those gringos are mine!' He says, motioning for the tourists to sit down.

'The food they sell is frozen,' warns the waiter next door.

The scene repeats over and over again. Most clients are visitors who decide to sit down for a drink to enjoy the ambiance. The problem begins with exorbitant prices, poor quality food and ridiculously small portions. Despite this, who wouldn't want to have a glass of wine and some tapas while enjoying views of Madrid's most famous landmark? For one day forget the cost, enjoy outdoor terraces and inviting cafes. Where else can you throw back a cold beer, admire 237 balconies while facing a 16th-century statue of the King Philip III on his horse?

The Plaza Mayor has a special relationship with old stamps. On a Sunday morning a coin and stamp market covers the perimeter of Plaza Mayor. Tables overflow with coins and stamps lined up in the colonnaded porticoes. Collectors are out in full force, most of them men in their fifties to eighties. Vendors and shoppers wear sweaters, quilted vests, tweed sport coats and perhaps a light scarf or jaunty cap in the chill of the shade. Connoisseurs huddle over tables, flipping through binders specially made to house collections. Some use magnifying glasses or lift their spectacles to bend down for a better look. No one was going to put one over on them. Small groups of men huddle together, discussing the merits or deficiencies of their finds. This scene has likely played out for decades.

NEARBY PUERTA DEL SOL IS ANOTHER OF MADRID'S WELL-KNOWN SPACES. Though it's not as breath taking as the Plaza Mayor, it does have some fun things to check out, like the bear statue, the clock tower, a fountain, the giant Tio Pepe sign, and the Kilometre Zero plaque.

The Tío Pepe sign advertising the famous brand of sherry, is unquestionably one of the capital's most characteristic sights. It is of symbolic value to Madrilenians. The Kilometre Zero plaque, the size of a flagstone might look simple, but Kilometre Zero is one of the most photographed spots in the country. Why? Well, it symbolises the point at which the country's six

radial roads begin. They connect the capital to Galicia, Extremadura, Andalusia, the Basque Country, Catalonia, and Valencia. The hub of Spain starts here. Roads radiate out, their distance in kilometres numbered from Zero.

There are many pedestrianized roads between Mayor and Sol. Street music, acrobatic performers, jugglers, and a Museum de Jamon too. This is not really tourism; it is simply a fun place to be. No admission fees, no staring at things fixed on walls, just friendly laughter. Surprisingly, there are some hidden places, not in the tourist books, close to the Sol.

CREATED AT THE BEGINNING OF THE 20th CENTURY, THE PARGUE DEL OESTE is home to a number of monuments and sights including the popular ancient Egyptian temple of Debod. During the Spanish Civil War, the park was also the site of the Battle of Ciudad Universitaria. Trenches and bunkers can still be visited to this day. Visitors to this lesser known area can check this out, a striking representation of war in a now peaceful area.

CASA HERNANZ FOOTWEAR 'Don't let the queue intimidate you. I waited about 40 min (came at 5:15pm). It was totally worth it! Everyone was extremely helpful and understanding. Spend the time in line to check out colours and styles to narrow a choice. I didn't feel pressured to rush and tried on a few. The basic unisex style is 9€. Very competitively priced and a great excuse to support a family business.'

PRINCIPE PIO: 'An awesome mall located in a train station which had been bombed and destroyed during the Spanish Civil War. Half of the building has since been rebuilt to be a train station and shopping mall. You can still see the bomb damage on the other half that sits abandoned. The shopping area has lots of little boutique shops which I have never seen of before. There are tons of eating options in the food court. Good place to stop at if you're tired of doing all the touristy stuff.'

ITS DISCERNING CLIENTAL will enjoy the ambiance of the Museo del Jamon. Many such outlets are situated in Madrid. Customers are mostly well-dressed office workers – businessmen in suits with open collar shirts and slim women attractively attired in smart outfits. Day trippers enter too. Younger people casually dressed in the latest sports gear, who stand excitedly as they look around slightly amazed.

The Museo del Jamon is an unusual name perhaps, influenced by dozens of legs of ham watching from above. Customers savour tapas and typical Spanish dishes which rely heavily on the best quality ham. These restaurants are large, with reasonable prices; hence are always full. There are quite a variety of dishes, well prepared, simple, matured ham, cheeses, cold cuts, artisan bread and an endless chilled display containing a large assortment of sandwiches and tapas. Have a good glass of wine, or a cool beer too.

SANTIAGO BERNABEU STADIUM: Lastly, before catching the AVE back home, rush across to this famous stadium, the home of Real Madrid Football Club. Have a photograph taken in the managers seat close to the touch line, but don't stand on the green stuff. Wave your arms about, shout, take a photograph, fantasize or dream – it's your day out, enjoy.

LOCATION - Madrid.
Map reference 40 2501 N, 3 4224 W. Capital of Spain

70. MALAGA
white villages, Picasso and ice cream

MALAGA IS A GATEWAY TO THE COSTA DEL SOL AND PLACES SUCH AS
Torremolinos, Estepona, Marbella and Puerto Banus. Thanks to about
300 days of sun each year, many British, American and Germans find
the Costa del Sol an agreeable place for retirement although summer
can be really hot with temperatures over 35 degrees.

Malaga is famous for La Alcazaba, a Moorish fortress palace, a
famous Roman Theatre and magnificent Cathedral. The Castillo de
Gibralfaro, a warlike fortress complete with towers and ramparts, sits
high above the city with fabulous views. Other places to visit are the
Museo del Vidrio, the Ataranzas Market set under a glass and iron roof,
the August Feria and of course its beaches and golf courses. If you
want to try street food that is completely local, then you can't go wrong
with espeto (grilled sardine) at a beachfront bar. The classic way to cook
this is to dig a hole in the sand, make a fire, then roast the sardines over
the embers on long, thick canes.

Malaga Province is scattered with Pueblos Blanco's, traditional,
picturesque white villages of closely packed old houses in narrow little
streets that mark the landscape like snowflakes. Though many of these
villages and small towns are firmly established on the tourist scene, they
have nevertheless retained their rural, Andalusian character.

Casares is one of the most ridiculously beautiful of all Andalusia's
white villages perched on top of a 1,427-foot-high cliff. Bizarrely,
given its vertiginous location, its attractiveness lies in the crunched up
together white house's which seem to have been stacked on top of each
another. Approaching Villanueva de la Concepcion through some of
Andalusia's most dramatic scenery, gives a superb view of this lovely
little village's privileged location. It resembles a giant patch of snow that
has somehow settled among endless olive groves and hills. Antequera,
known as 'The Heart of Andalusia', has kept its pueblo blanco style
atmosphere despite its considerable size.

Malaga is also a gateway to Ronda. Were it not perched on two sides of a 330-foot-deep gorge; the beautiful country village of Ronda would probably be overlooked by many visitors to Malaga. But it's beautiful and slightly terrifying bridge, built in the 18th century to join up Ronda's two halves, is an architectural masterpiece that has made this quiet little town a most visited destination in Andalusia.

While Malaga provides a new home for foreign residents, the opportunity to visit white villages, Ronda and the Camino del Rey (covered elsewhere in this book) its largely hidden charm involves following the footsteps of Pablo Picasso.

IN FACT, THERE ARE MANY THINGS ABOUT PICASSO IN THIS CITY.

The city is absolutely devoted to its most famous citizen, a native of Malaga. There is the museum, a house and a statue located in the main square Plaza de la Merced.

Pablo Picasso had to be an artist. He grew up between the brushes and teachings of his father and because he showed a nimble mind with a skilful hand for painting. His name began to be heard in 1898 with his first solo exhibition. As a professional artist, Picasso would immerse himself in the bohemian and artistic environment of Paris causing him to explore his own style, going from a famous blue period to a pink period, then cubism, surrealism and expressionism.

Some of his works, such as 'The Young Ladies of Avignon', were a real shock to a society that did not fit with the new pictorial styles that were emerging and in many cases completely experimental.

Guernica

Perhaps he is most remembered by the painting 'Guernica', the immense oil on canvas that he drew in 1937 as a denouncement of the bombing suffered by the Basque population and the atrocities committed in civil war. Beyond painting, Picasso, like Dali, cultivated other artistic fields such as sculpture, set design or engravings.

Picasso's success is a melting pot of many factors: his genius, the schools where he studied (mainly Barcelona and Paris), his interest in social life, friendships with artists and dealers, a prolific production of paintings, an innovative mindset and his leadership. At the end of his career he tended to paint increasingly simple figures, bordering on abstract, but his authority as an artist was then unquestionable. Picasso earned the right to break the rules, as he mastered them perfectly.

A man of simple tastes, with a great fondness for the Mediterranean sun and bullfighting, he had a complicated sentimental life with two wives and numerous lovers. He continued working until his death in 1973 in France at 91 years of age.

MALAGA'S GASTRONOMY IS EATING ICE CREAM AT MIDNIGHT. When one thinks about delicious ice cream, often the word gelatto comes to mind. But in Malaga, more and more artisan ice cream shops are popping up, where they make creamy, soft, delicious ice cream. *Helado* is the word in Spanish, and if you don't know it by heart at the start of a visit you definitely will when you leave.

In the city centre after dinner you will find many ice-cream shops open. In fact, most ice-cream corner shops during the weekend close at 3.00 am. Have you ever experienced a midnight ice-cream? Try the most popular flavours, like leche merengada, vanilla, turron or seasonal fruits.

In summer, the days are long, the heat constant; this sweet treat cools down body temperatures, satisfies cravings and can easily be taken twice a day!

We all know, when the best ingredients are used, the final product is amazing. So, it doesn't come as a surprise to know all the best ice cream in Malaga is made with natural ingredients. They also have a large selection of flavours and options for food allergies and vegans. A special mention goes to turron ice cream. Nougat is an immensely popular flavour because the main ingredient is almonds. This nut is produced in the fields around Malaga; hence it is also used in all types of local cuisine.

LOCATIONS – all close together in Andalusia.
Malaga.
Map reference 36 4328 N, 4 2509 W.
Antequera, one of the white villages.
Map reference 37 0127 N, 4 3340 W.
Ronda.
Map reference 36 4534 N, 5 0952 W.

71. PYRENEES
National Park of Ordesa and Monte Perdido

THERE ARE FIFTEEN NATIONAL PARKS IN SPAIN: ten in the Iberian Peninsula, four in the Canary Islands and one in the Balearic Islands. The National Park of Ordesa y Monte Perdido in the Pyrnees tops the list, being one of the world's first national parks created in 1918. Today, it's a magical place to visit, filled with soaring peaks, glacial lakes, cascading waterfalls and all manner of flora and fauna. An environment that seems like real paradise. The park can be found approximately 12km north of the Spanish city of Huesca. There are connections to Ordesa and the town of Ainsa. It is a UNESCO World Heritage Site.

Covering 156km² it is made up of a variety of different zones – from high massifs to glacial valleys, to rivers and waterfalls. One of the most attractive areas is the Ordesa Valley, after which the park is named, which is crossed by the Rio Arazas River.

The Park is filled with stunning natural attractions, some of which include ancient glacial lakes. One of the most spectacular is Lake Marbore, close to the Monte Perdido peak. A highlight is the Cola de Caballo, or Horsetail Waterfall, located in a natural rock amphitheatre. It's quite a sight to behold, with many high-level water cascades.

At the centre stands the magnificent summit of Monte Perdido itself; at 3,355m it's the third highest peak in the Pyrenees. The park is filled with many different hiking trails of varying levels of length and difficulty. There are trails in high rocky pinnacles, and those down in the lush valleys, or around the edge of lakes.

There are a number of adventure sports visitors can enjoy. Excursions by 4×4, two different horse-riding stables and companies offering

kayaking, white water rafting and canyoning. One of the best activities is without a doubt, canyoning. It is a perfect sport to delve deep into mountains and rivers, to enjoy an exciting experience unloading adrenaline.

Stay overnight in the park. There are many different options, both near and in the park itself. Choose from rural guesthouses, shelters (refugios), campsites, hotels and hostels. Even better, try the unusual town of Ainsa, close by.

THE MEDEVIAL TOWN OF AINSA IS FOUND AT THE SPECTACULAR CONFLUENCE of the Ara and Cinca rivers, under the watchful eye of Pena Montanesa. It's an old town where time seems to have stopped in the Middle Ages. With most towns the Plaza Mayor is in the centre. Not so Ainsa. This nerve centre sits to one side, high up in the remains of a castle where every summer, the Castillo de Aínsa International Music Festival is held.

This entire urban complex maintains a medieval flavour and has been declared a Historic-Artistic Complex. To walk through its streets is to enter more than a thousand years of existence. Pass by various emblazoned houses, stone walls, cobbled streets, the castle, the Plaza Mayor and the church of Santa María. This is a magical town that visits another era. A charming square, full of balconies, flowers and medieval arcades.

LOCATIONS – both in the Eastern Pyrenees close to Andorra.

Ordesa valley, Huesca, Aragon Pyrenees.

Map reference 42 3916 N, 0 0320 W.

Ainsa, Huesca, Aragon Pyrenees. (on the edge of the National Park)

Map reference 42 24 53 N. 0 0825 E.

72. TOLEDO

swords and mizipan

TOLEDO'S HISTORIC CENTRE IS WHERE A GLORIOUS PAST IS GREETED AT EVERY TURN. The old city is a cross-fertilisation of Jewish, Islamic and Christian cultures. In many buildings these influences are blended together. Try to find your way around labyrinthine streets that are enclosed by historic walls, defended gates and fortified bridges that stand proudly tall. Imagine Spanish Kings who ruled an entire great empire from Toledo.

Toledo's Cathedral is one of the most important places to visit. So too is the Alcazar located on the highest part of the city. The Monastery de San Juan de los Reyes is again a classic construction. A medieval bridge, known as Puente de San Martín, is built over the Tajo river being one of Toledo's iconic symbols. From this bridge there is an excellent panorama of the old town; it is a very romantic place to go for an evening walk. Toledo has a museum dedicated to El Greco, one of the most important and influential Spanish artists of all time. Good guides to these impressive buildings can best be obtained from the many tourist books available.

One of the most special things to do in Toledo is to explore it by night when the city acquires a completely different air: lights turn on and point at main buildings, creating beautiful effects.

ONE PRODUCT TOLEDO HAS BEEN RENOWNED FOR IS STEEL. Famous for high-quality alloy that is remarkably durable, steel is flexible enough to be made into swords.

Toledo became a centre of traditional sword-making and Toledo swords became the standard weaponry in medieval times. The result was a sturdy, superior quality sword suitable for heavily armoured armies. The Carthaginian General Hannibal Barca used the Toledo blade to defeat the Romans, who at the time were using inferior bronze swords.

The Romans later adopted the Toledo sword as they spread through the Iberian peninsula. All European armies knew about the superior quality of Toledo steel so in other parts of the world craftsmen tried to imitate the Toledo product, but they failed. The sword became particularly important in the 16th and 17th centuries when Spain was a global power and Toledo one of its most-prized imperial cities.

But by the end of the 18th century, the importance of Toledo and its famed weapon began to dwindle. Given the rise of munitions in war, the sword was then used for ceremonial purposes. Blacksmiths were no longer sought after to forge blades made from Toledo steel, and slowly the art diminished. How to tell a real Toledo sword from a fake? The Toledo product will be perfectly balanced, its blade will be marked by small blemishes that show where a mallet struck it with varying degrees of force. The edge of a fake mass-produced sword is completely smooth because it is shaped by a machine, which can regulate the strength of its strikes.

Before the age of modern movie workshops, classic film producers in Hollywood are said to have sourced their metal props and swords from Toledo swordsmiths. They commissioned specific designs, but many were impossible to make. Today elaborate swords for movies are made of plastic.

Toledo now resembles something of a medieval playground. Many commercial shops have capitalized on the city's rich history, selling medieval trinkets and sword replicas. Tourists love the sword; customs officials do not.

MARZIPAN IS A CULINARY ART IN TOLEDO. WATCH THE PRONUNCIATION, ITS CALLED MAZIPAN, NOT MARZIPAN. The city's

most beloved confectionary is delightfully balanced and not too sweet. Elsewhere in Spain, marzipan usually comes in the form of a traditional Christmas cake, but here you find it sold as a daily snack.

Mazipan is made from almond paste traditionally made to resemble cute animals. While the Italian version of this sweet is usually made into

the shape of various fruits, Toledo's mazipan comes in a huge variety of shapes such as little pigs, bears, and crescent moons.

LOCATION

Toledo, Castille la Mancha.
Map reference 39 5147 N, 4 0194 W. Regional capital

73. VALL DE NURIA
by rack and pinion

VALL DE NURIA, A MOUNTAIN RESORT EAST OF ANDORRA, MUST BE SPAIN'S BEST KEPT SECRET. At 3000 metres above sea level, in a perfect little valley it is hidden from view by surrounding mountains. Spectacular, stunning, awesome, breath-taking, beautiful and jaw-dropping.

The Nuria valley is a summer and winter resort high in Pyrenees. This is rugged open country, much cooler than the foothills below. Accessibility is by a new, modern, rack and pinion railway taking 40 minutes from Ribes de Freser which also has car parking and main line  train connections. An alternative is to drive to Queralbs halfway up the line and take the rack and pinion from there. On one side of the rail track is a trail to Nuria (in one direction some 2 hours) and on the other side a fast tumbling river.

Arriving at the top of the valley, a quite austere semi-circular building, reminiscent of those lining a high street plaza, comes into view. To some extent it looks like a huge great monastery but not so. It is used for feeding visitors, having a toilet break, and sheltering from high-altitude sun. The building contains a hotel, exhibition centre, restaurants and is a focal point for many activities. In a way it adds to a stunning impact, contrasting emerald pastures with deep winter snow and a sparkling lake.

In summer, the range of activities include long walking trails which wind their way through the rugged snow-capped mountains. There are ten marked trails with a few around 2km. Alternatively head up one of the trails which climbs above the valley to a peak, or a coll, or even to France, a trip well worth the effort to enjoy panoramic views of this valley at its impressive best. Look out for Marmots and if you're lucky, Pyrenean Chamois.

LOCATIONS – Gerona, Eastern Pyrenees. Close to Andorra.

Vall de Nuria.

Map reference 42 2350 N, 2 0911 E.

Ribes de Freser.

Map reference 42 1821 N, 2 1005 E.

PEOPLE

74. ALMERIA
cowboy country

THOUSANDS OF FILM AND ADVERTISING SHOOTS HAVE TAKEN PLACE IN TABERNAS DESERT which has led it to be known as 'European Hollywood'. Some of the most prestigious actors and directors in the world of cinema have passed through its arid landscapes, such as Steven Spielberg, Sergio Leone, Clint Eastwood, Sean Connery, Harrison Ford, Sophia Loren, Arnold Schwarzenegger, and a lot more too.

In the Tabernas desert, a few kilometres from the Natural Park Cabo de Gata-Nijar, are redesigned villages of the Wild West used in many western movies. Film producers found in this desert a setting of unique natural beauty that accurately reproduces the landscapes of the North American wild west culture. They built sets and small towns depicted in western movies.

Film making began here in the late 50s, with the 60s and 70s having the largest number of productions. A decline began in the 1980s, but a good number of films continued to be shot. Currently, many video clips and television commercials are shot here, and occasionally a movie or series that takes advantage of the sets and hours of light that Almería offers. In total more than 300 films have been filmed, mostly westerns.

The Tabernas rose to stardom thanks to director Sergio Leone who filmed the mythical trilogy of the dollar starring Clint Eastwood - *For a Handful of Dollars, Death had a Price* and *The Good, the Bad and the Ugly.*

He also shot the classic *Until Its Time Came*, with Claudia Cardinale and Henry Fonda. Besides films from the Wild West, great productions such as *Cleopatra*, *Patton*, *Lawrence of Arabia*, *Indiana Jones and the Last Crusade*, have all been filmed here.

Today the film sets have been transformed into three theme parks.

Fort Bravo Texas Hollywood: The facilities that you can find here are a Sheriff's office, a bank, a funeral home, a telegraph office, a barbershop and other buildings of the American West. It also has a film museum, a museum of cars and stagecoaches, a cactus garden and a Indian children's park. Show time is where cowboys fight with their fists, drag the good guy on the ground and hang the bad guy.

Oasys Mini Hollywood: This set was designed by Carlo Simi and built for Sergio Leone for his huge successes. After the last film, extras employed on the project decided to buy the set and turn it into a visitor attraction. Today it belongs to a group of hotels. The park features daily cowboy performances, such as a simulated raid and a re-enactment of Jesse James' final moments. The complex also has swimming pools, an abandoned gold mine, a cowboy-style lounge, a fun barn for children's activities and many souvenir shops with western costumes and objects.

Western Leone: It is the smallest of the three desert theme parks in Tabernas. Western Leone was originally built to shoot the movie *Hasta que llego su Hora* (1968). The great red house, around which much of the film's scenes revolve, remains an attraction, along with other buildings in a typical western city. In 1970, a fortress was built, this structure was used as a film set for *El Condor* and subsequent films. Like the other parks, a show from the West, recreating the fights between good and bad, takes place.

LOCATION

Tabernas, Almeria.
Map reference 37 0018 N, 2 2656 W.
Nearest large town - Almeria

75. BURGOS
Sergio Leone and sad hill cemetery

WISH TO SEE CLINT EASTWOOD, LEE VAN CLEEF AND ELI WALLACH AGAIN? Then come to Burgos and relive it like a cowboy from the American West; you will freak out!

Sad Hill Cemetery was built between the Burgos municipalities of Contreras and Santo Domingo de Silos to shoot the final scene of the movie *The Good, the Bad and the Ugly*. This is where the 15-minute classic movie scene was shot and in Burgos you can relive the scene at Sad Hill Cemetery.

It was the summer of 1966 when the Italian film director Sergio Leone was in Spain locating exterior settings. Leone had already shot some of his famous spaghetti westerns in the Tabernas Desert in Almeria. The film he was shooting needed a stage with a bridge and a river, something he would hardly find in the province of Almería. He found it in the Arlanza river valley, in the Sierra de la Demanda.

The Monastery of San Pedro de Arlanza was transformed into the Mission San Antonio. Near the municipality of Carazo, the unionist Fort Betterville was erected. The Arlanza river became the Rio Grande's Langstone Bridge. In the Mirandilla Valley, remarkably close to Santo Domingo de Silos, the Sad Hill Cemetery was built where the final scene of the film was shot.

Leone had the help of the Spanish army to build the circular Sad Hill Cemetery. More than 5,000 'graves' were created. Most of them had their own wooden cross. After finishing filming the place was abandoned. Over the years, vegetation covered the 'graves'; the wooden crosses rotted.

In 2013, with the intention of recovering the film scenes for tourism purposes, the Sad Hill Cultural Association emerged. Its members took months to unearth the cemetery's original central cobblestone. Two years later, on the fiftieth anniversary of the shooting of the film, the association began to recover 'graves' in the cemetery. Thousands of volunteers cleared vegetation and breathed new life into this gigantic setting.

Since 2016, the association has managed to recover more than 1,500 'graves.' It has done so thanks to a somewhat macabre patronage campaign. For only 15 euros, anyone could have a headstone with a name in Sad Hill Cemetery. This original campaign spread across the globe, with requests coming from everywhere. An American fan of the film even tried to have his ashes deposited here after his death. Among the tombs that already have a name is one dedicated to the director Sergio Leone, another to the unknown soldier. The financial success was astonishing – it is now closed.

The access track that goes to Sad Hill cemetery is three kilometres from Contreras and four from Santo Domingo de Silos. Once there the cemetery is open to visitors. Take time to stroll among the endless rows of crosses. Discover inscriptions that will surprise.

LOCATION

Sad Hill Cemetery, Castille & Leon.
Map reference 41 5925 N, 3 2431 W.
Nearest large town - Burgos

76. FIGUERES
Dali, genius, or a tortured mind

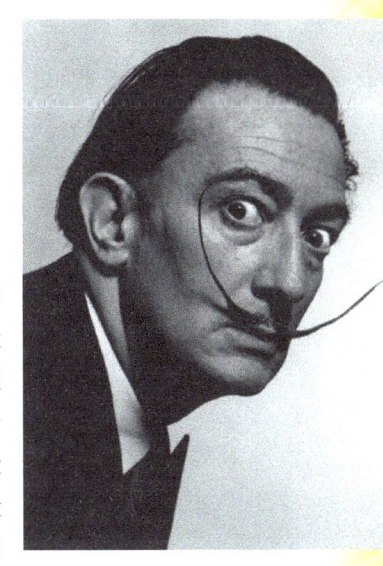

FIGUERES IS NOT THE SORT OF PLACE TO LOCATE AN INTERNATIONAL MUSEUM, but Dali was different. A museum not in a capital city? A museum standing proud, brazenly saying 'come and look at me, it does not matter where I am.' It is one Spain's most visited attractions. Not exactly hidden Spain! But unusual, off the beaten track and as many say, controversial.

The location of the Dali Museum, on the main road north from Barcelona to Perpignan, close to holiday resorts along the Costa Brava and near the French border, was the choice of Dali. Specifically, it was the former Municipal Theatre of Figueres. Destroyed in a fire at the end of the Spanish Civil War, the building was left to rot. Dali wanted to take advantage of the 'charm' offered by the ruins of the former theatre to house his museum.

How ironical it is to know that Dali rests here, hidden from today's visitors for he is buried in a crypt below the museum, under a part that was the old theatre's stage floor. Perhaps complete with paint, brushes and a supply of men's hair wax preparation?

What is the attraction of the Dali Museum? The answer lies in the uniqueness of what is seen, the perplexing images of a tortured mind, the creativity of a Spanish genius all displayed in what can only be described as totally unsuitable surroundings. The popularity of this place causes problems for Figueres; it has narrow streets. Coaches and cars are competing for parking spaces. People stand in a gigantic queue, under a hot sun, for the privilege of walking nose to tail round an exhibition.

Upon entering the museum there is literature everywhere, most of it written in an attempt to explain Dali's mind when creating his paintings and sculptures. There is however an issue, explained by this quote from the great painter himself.

'The fact that I myself, at the moment of painting, do not understand my own pictures does not mean that these pictures have no meaning; on the contrary, their meaning is so profound, complex, coherent, and involuntary that it escapes the simplest analysis of logical intuition.'

Now that is revealing – if Dali does not know what, who, or why, he is painting do we mortals have any chance of understanding it? Study one of his greatest, well documented paintings:

Soft Construction with Boiled Beans (1936).

Dali painted this masterpiece six months before the Spanish Civil War began. He claimed to have been aware of the war due to 'the prophetic power of his subconscious mind'. The painting reflects his anxiety during the time and predicts the horror and violence in war. It portrays two bodies, one darker than the other, in a gruesome fight where neither appears to be a victor. The monstrous creature is self-destructive just as a civil war is. The boiled beans in the painting, which are also mentioned in the title, are perhaps a reference to the simple stew that was eaten by poor citizens living through a difficult time.

Let's try sculptures. Two sculptures remarkably popular during his surrealist phase are the Lobster Telephone and the Mae West Lips Sofa. Believe it or not, the lobster telephone actually did work. While it is not on display in the museum, many Salvador Dali sculptures are, including near the entrance, the famous Mae West Lips Sofa. As the story goes, Dali was quite taken by the actress Mae West and inspired to create this piece. The sofa was built in the shape of her lips. Visitors are not allowed to touch or sit on it.

Dalí was renowned for his flamboyant personality, being a mischievous provocateur, as well as his undeniable technical virtuosity. He is among the most versatile and prolific artists of the 20th century and the most famous Surrealist. Though chiefly remembered for his painting and sculpture output, in the course of his long career he successfully turned to printmaking, fashion, advertising, writing and, perhaps most unknown, filmmaking with Alfred Hitchcock.

UNDERSTANDABLY DALI DID NOR RESIDE IN FIGUERES. He lived not too far away in Cadaques, a hidden coastal gem, just visible on a map at the easternmost point in Spain. Its implausibly azure-blue waters and piercing sunlight famously drew painters such as Magritte, Matisse and Picasso, as well its adopted son Salvador Dalí. Set around a remote bay in the Costa Brava, the town's pebble beach waterfront and patchwork of steep, narrow streets are a world away from the unrestrained package-holiday resorts along this coast. Getting there is via a treacherous coastal road that winds and dips. Those who make it are rewarded with stunning cliff-edge walks, a rustic, pebbly, picture book waterfront, set in one of the most unspoilt villages of the Mediterranean. Just the spot for a painter.

LOCATIONS – both close to the French border.

Figueres, Girona.
Map reference 42 1556 N, 2 5729 E.

Cadaques, Girona.
Map reference 42 1720 N, 3 1640 E.

77. TWO BRITISH HEROES
path, street and bust

THE GEORGE ORWELL ROUTE IS A RECREATED PATH THROUGH THE CIVIL WAR. Famed English author George Orwell headed to Spain during the Spanish Civil War in order to join the fight for democracy, mainly out of idealism. Today, his path through Aragon is remembered by a trail of recreated fortifications.

Orwell joined the fighting in the Spanish Civil War in 1936, despite the reasoned advice of fellow author, Henry Miller. Despite being a volunteer, Orwell wanted to head to the front line, but it was not to be. Instead, he was sent with his regiment to Aragon, where fighting was light. He didn't see much action there, but he did encounter a great deal of hardship among soldiers, including hunger and terrible living

conditions. While his initial visit was uneventful, he would return to Aragon later only to be shot in the neck. He survived and his ordeal would be described in his book *Homage to Catalonia*.

Despite a general agreement among many in Spain to let the civil war be buried in the past, many of the trenches and fortifications where Orwell spent time have been methodically recreated. The battlefield along what is now called the George Orwell Route looks as if had never even been touched by time, much less war. Visitors can now walk the same hilltop path that was not only visited by Orwell, but by countless soldiers who took part in this tragic war. The Spanish Civil War may not be a popular subject among many, but thanks to Orwell's high-profile visit, this battlefield will not be forgotten at any time soon.

ARCHIBALD DICKSON IS A NAME KNOWN BETTER IN ALICANTE THAN IN HIS CARDIFF HOME. He became a sailor and later a captain on international voyages. During the Spanish Civil War, Dickson captained various ships in 1938 that brought supplies to Republican Spain. As a blockade runner in 1939, he took over the *SS Stanbrook* owned by the shipping company France Navigation. On March 17th he received orders to set sail for Alicante to pick up a shipment of tobacco, saffron and oranges for Algeria.

However, he found close to a thousand Republican refugees who, in the face of the imminent fall of the Republic, requested to go with him to Algeria. Most of them were waiting for other ships that never came. Dickson had orders not to board anyone except for reasons of 'force majeure', but for humanitarian reasons he decided to allow them to board leaving the cargo behind. The number of people who wished to board quickly began to increase. Dickson began to fear for the stability of the ship and even considered removing the gangway, but ultimately did not.

With about 2,500 people on board, the *Stanbrook* left Alicante on March 28 towards Oran as this route was believed to be clear of Francoist ships. Just 10 minutes later, an aerial bombardment began over the city that was seen by all the ship's occupants.

Due to overcrowding, the *Stanbrook* was on several occasions at risk of capsizing, especially when other ships passed. The next day he managed to reach Oran. However, the authorities there did not give them authorization to anchor, so they stayed another night on board with little food for so many people in precarious sanitary conditions. After several comings and goings, Dickson finally managed to obtain permission for landing women and children. Men had to wait almost a month.

After this episode Dickson returned to the UK. A few months later, World War II began and the *Stanbook* was used again as a supply ship. Just eight months after the feat at Alicante, Dickson was commissioned to bring supplies to France but on the way, near Dunkerque, a German submarine torpedoed the *Stanbrook*, killing all of its crew, including captain Dickson.

At the Boghari concentration camp in Algeria, where most of the

Stanbrook refugees were located, the news came. A minute's silence was observed.

Years later, in 2009 a tribute was organized in Alicante. In this city, a street was named after his ship *Stanbrook*. The ship was the last to set sail from Republican soil carrying refugees before the final fall of the Republic. Archibald Dickson's action has been compared to the German businessman Schindler, who saved the lives of 1,200 Jews during the Holocaust.

In Alicante, he is remembered as a hero. In 2014 a memorial bust of the captain was installed on the quayside to honour him. It was unveiled almost exactly 75 years after the ship set sail from the port of Alicante.

LOCATIONS

George Orwell Route, Aragon.

Map reference 41 4906 N, 0 3033 W.

Nearest large town Zaragoza.

Archibald Dickson, Alicante.

Map reference 38 2407 N, 0 2925 W. Capital of region

78. MOJACAR AND BENIDORM
two Spanish visionaries

QUEEN ISABELLA, HERNANDO CORTES, PABLO PICASSO, Diego Velazquez, Penelope Cruz, and Rafael Nadal are some of Spain's influential people. It's a personal choice of course. Some people are not famous, simply influential. People operating under the radar, unknown, unremembered, unsung. People like Mayor Jacinto Alarcon and Pedro Zaragoza Oils. People whose vision had a significant impact on modern Spain.

DEPOPULATION OF MOJACAR BEGAN IN THE MID NINETEENTH CENTURY and started to assume alarming proportions after the end of the Civil War. By this time drought had become so chronic, fishing boats were gradually disappearing from its foreshore. By 1960, Mojacar had a population of less than 1,000 whereas at the turn of the century it had been around 8,000. Before leaving emigrants ripped doors, windows, and beams from their houses to help pay for their traveling expenses. Their homes stood like empty skeletons in deserted streets.

Mojacar would have ended there if it were not for the Mayor, Jacinto Alarcon, who set about publicising its regional attractions. In this, he was helped by a group of writers and artists who, captivated by its charms, had chosen Mojacar as their home. They dug wells in search of water to irrigate fields. The ruined houses were gradually demolished, plots of land were given away on the condition that new houses were immediately built. All kinds of amenities were extended to those who wanted to become residents.

Would enough people come to see Mojacar? Jacinto knew so long as people came, Mojacar itself would do the rest. And so, it was. The village's charm captivated all those who visited. In 1962, Mojacar was a curious sight. Everywhere were mounds of cement, sand, and lime. In its streets, lorries lumbered ceaselessly up and down the hills, donkeys trundled along carrying water, workmen's voices relayed orders from one construction site to another, cranes and pulleys creaked incessantly.

And so Mojacar rose from the shell of its former self. Attractive white house's now cover a hill giving a honeycombed effect. Artists, writers, musicians, archaeologists, businessmen and diplomats have their summer residences in Mojacar. One of the streets is appropriately called Ambassadors Row.

Meanwhile, due to Jacinto Alarcon, Mojacar continues to make progress and is aptly called 'The Pearl of Almeria'. Golf courses, apartment blocks and major developments occur around a town, which 40 years ago was crumbling into extinction.

'THIS IS THE VERY SPOT WHERE I WAS BORN ON MAY 15, 1922',

said Pedro Zaragoza Oils pointing downwards to an imaginary bed that occupied a spot in their family home. The house eventually made way for a block of shops, offices and apartments that became part of an urban plan which took a village of 1,500 souls to a city which is now the major holiday destination of Europe. It's called Benidorm.

Guidebooks state Benidorm was originally a fishing port, but that was never the case, although villagers did live off the sea. 'When you have no fresh water and the land is only fit for olives and almonds, you eat a lot of fish!' exclaims Pedro. Many men in the village travelled the world on liners and cargo ships. They knew they could make a better way of life. So why not tourism? 'What else? All we had was the sun, sea and beaches.'

By the 60s, visitors from northern Europe were beginning to arrive in droves. The icon of liberty was a bikini, its roomy bottom and bra top barely recognisable in comparison to today's string and handkerchief affairs. But Spain was held in a grip of the Catholic Church; this scanty garment was a tool of the devil.

In one famous incident, a British tourist, sitting in a bar opposite the beach wearing only a bikini was told by a Guardia Civil officer that she wasn't allowed to wear it. She hit him! Her strike for social justice resulted in a fine of 4,000 pesetas, no mean sum when the average wage was just over 100 pesetas a day. Step forward Pedro Zaragoza. 'If you want people to come to your town for their holidays you have to accommodate their culture as well. People have to feel free to wear what they want. If they enjoy themselves, they will not only come back, but will tell their friends to come too.'

So when Pedro Zaragoza took his 'War of the Bikini' to General Franco everyone thought he was mad, but he gained his audience who decreed visitors could wear a bikini in the streets and plazas of Benidorm, the first town in Spain where they were allowed to do so. The truth of the matter was simple, the bikini saved the economy of Spain and launched a tourist superstrate it is today.

Pedro Zaragoza's greatest achievement was the Plan General de Ordenacion de Benidorm which he brought into being in February 1954. This was an urban revolution. 'Many landowners were noticeably short sighted, couldn't understand why, for example, I wanted an avenue 80 metres wide. Their objections were hardly surprising considering there were only seven cars in the town at the time. They thought 10 metres was enough. So, we eventually settled on 40.'

In the Plan was every building would have an area of surrounding leisure land. So, whilst Benidorm gained a reputation as being a high rise development, seen from the air it is in fact very green and open. The plan is still in use today. Now Benidorm boasts more hotel rooms than the whole of Greece. It is arguably the most important holiday destination in Europe. And you can still go fishing!

LOCATIONS

Mojacar, Almeria.
Map reference 37 0825 N, 1 5102 W.

Benidorm, Alicante Province.
Map reference 38 3228 N, 0 0720 W.

79. VALENCIA
marriage, wabi-sabi style

THE STANDOUT MARBLE QUARRY IN SPAIN IS LOCATED AT PINISO, ALICANTE. It is the largest marble quarry anywhere in the world. However, far removed from industrial quarrying, an abandoned marble quarry near Valencia sets the stage for Wabi-Sabi inspired weddings.

Unusual wedding locations are every couple's dream, but what does wabi-sabi mean? It is the Japanese art of finding beauty in imperfection, accepting the natural cycle of growth, decay, and death. It is simple, slow and uncluttered, embracing authenticity above all. Wabi-sabi is flea markets, not warehouse stores; aged wood, not laminate; rice paper, not glass. It celebrates cracks and crevices and the marks of time. It's a reminder of all transient things on this planet, our bodies as well as the material world around us are in the process of returning to the dust from which we came. Wabi-sabi embraces liver spots, rust, and frayed edges. It is underplayed and modest, the kind of quiet, undeclared beauty that waits patiently to be discovered. A richly mellow beauty that's striking but not obvious, one to have around for a long, long time. Its peace found in a moss garden, the musty smell of geraniums, the astringent taste of powdered green tea. Got it!

One of the coolest things about marriage or eloping is that people can venture to more remote places, in lieu of finding a city venue, or a castle which can accommodate a large celebration. So, an abandoned marble quarry in Valencia is just that: dilapidated, natural, and unconventional. The quarry, remarkably close to the  sea, was abandoned in the '80s because the marble was not pure enough and contained many fossil remains - which is perfect for the wabi-sabi ideal. It's all about finding the beauty within marble imperfections and accepting the cycle of growth and decay.

You can say your vows here, but before that some planning is required by one of several local wedding companies. To complement the vast marble slabs, unstructured floral compositions are required to blend with tons of natural materials making sure everything remains authentic. It's the wabi-sabi movement, creating a mood encompassing the feeling of simplicity, natural essence, contact with nature, prime materials, and moody dress colours.

LOCATION – this quarry can only be visited by organisations such as Wedding Companies.

Other books by Harry King

How to Buy a Home in Spain - How to Books - 2nd edition
Spain – Your Guide to a New Life - How to Books - 2nd edition
Buy to Let Spain - How to Books
Knowing the Law in Spain – How to Books
Gonzalez – the son of his father – Libro's International

Lightning Source UK Ltd.
Milton Keynes UK
UKHW021222140622
404398UK00002B/7